THE PATH OF GOD

BY REVEREND CAROL RUTH KNOX, PH.D.

COY F. CROSS II, PH.D.
EDITOR

Koho Pono, LLC

THE PATH OF GOD

Published by Koho Pono, LLC
Clackamas, Oregon USA; http://KohoPono.com

The right to publish the works of Carol Ruth Knox is licensed by Coy F. Cross II through an agreement with Unity of Walnut Creek. All of Carol Ruth Knox's work is owned and copyrighted by Unity of Walnut Creek.

Copyright © 2013 Coy F. Cross II, Ph.D., All Rights Reserved

No part of this publication may be reproduced, stored in or introduced into a retrieval system, or transmitted in any form or by any means (electronic, mechanical, photocopying, recording, scanning or otherwise) without the prior written permission of the publisher. Requests for permission should be directed to the Permissions Department, Koho Pono, LLC, info@kohopono.com.

First Paperback Edition 17july2013
Library of Congress Control Number: 2013911285

ISBN: 978-1-938282-07-2 (trade paper)
ISBN: 978-1-938282-09-6 (eBook)

Manufactured in the United States of America

"I loved Carol's teachings... I was immediately drawn to them from the first time that I heard and read them. She was the beginning of my knowing that I also was a mystic."

- Dr. Marj Britt, Senior Minister, Unity of Tustin

"Carol Ruth Knox will take you from the mundane to the metaphysical as you read her words. She was a spiritually gifted teacher who used her own growth as stepping stones to teach the path of God. She was a mentor and great friend whose love of life was shared by all. I loved her deeply."

- Jo Coudray, Member, Unity of Walnut Creek

"As a Unity Minister of 27 years and a psychotherapist of 35, I have met 100s of teachers whose teachings have influenced me. However, only a few remain in an inner circle of influence and they are always with me and guiding me along the way: Rev. Carol Ruth Knox is one of these people."

- Rev. Suzanne Carter, M.A., L.P.C., Unity Minister, 1986

DEDICATION

I dedicate this book to Carol Ruth Knox, my mentor and my friend and to Carol Martha Cross—my beloved and muse.

Acknowledgements

I am grateful: to Reverend David McArthur, Senior Minister at Unity of Walnut Creek, and the Center's Board of Directors for granting me the license for this material; to my publishers, Scott Burr and Dayna Hubenthal of Koho Pono, LLC, for their professional help, constant advice, and support; to my friend Gail Derin for her editorial expertise; to my family for their continued love and support; and especially to my late wife Carol for her encouragement and unfailing belief in me.

Carol Ruth Knox Biography

Carol Ruth Knox was born in Somerville, Massachusetts, near Boston, on December 16, 1938. She graduated cum laude from Tufts University in Medford, Massachusetts, receiving a Bachelor of Arts degree in Music and in English. She completed a Master of Arts degree in Musicology from Brown University in Providence, Rhode Island. Carol Ruth's doctoral degree was awarded by the California Institute of Integral Studies—San Francisco. Her dissertation explored the Prayer of the Heart, an ancient form of Christian meditation.

Prior to entering the Unity ministry, Carol Ruth taught English and Music and was Director of Music at a high school in Connecticut. She was also a Director of the Massachusetts Association for the Adult Blind.

Between 1955 and 1968 Carol Ruth toured the eastern United States as a professional concert pianist.

As a lifetime student of Unity, she completed her first Unity class in Cambridge, Massachusetts, under the guidance of the Reverend Edna Titus.

She attended Unity School for Religious Studies, Unity Village, Missouri from 1968 to 1970, and was ordained as a Unity minister on Aug. 14, 1970 by the Association of Unity Churches.

Carol Ruth became minister of the Unity Center of Walnut Creek in California soon after her ordination. Taking a small group, she developed it into one of the largest ministries west of the Mississippi with nearly 400 active members. She served as the Center's minister until her death nearly seventeen years later.

Reverend Knox authored many Unity publications, lectured widely on the West Coast of the USA to professional and service clubs, conducted seminars, appeared on weekly television and radio series, and wrote a newspaper column. She conducted workshops and taught classes throughout Unity and was also deeply engaged in the greater community thereby making a positive impact in the world.

On February 1, 1987, Reverend Carol Ruth Knox was killed by an intruder in her home in Antioch, California, thus ending the life of a visionary and living example of God's Love. Her legacy of passion, wisdom, and faith continues to change the lives of everyone who reads or hears her words.

TABLE OF CONTENTS

INTRODUCTION 1

1: THE PATH OF GOD 7

2: THE PATH OF COURAGE 23

3: THE PATH OF EVOLUTION 41

4: THE PATH OF LOVE (CHERISH) 63

5: THE PATH OF LOVE (THE SHADOW) 79

6: THE PATH OF NON-DUALITY 101

7: THE PATH OF MEDITATION 125

8: THE PATH OF PRAYER 143

9: THE PATH OF THE HEART 163

10: THE PATH OF NON-RESISTANCE 183

11: THE PATH OF DEATH & RESURRECTION 207

ENGAGE WITH COY F. CROSS II 225

Koho Pono LLC 231

INTRODUCTION

As a child in Southeastern Kentucky, Baptist and Adventist Christian churches shaped my vision of God, prayer, the world, and my place in it. I later became the teenaged-thorn in the side of my ministers and elders, constantly questioning church teachings. Never finding adequate answers and feeling a deep sense of guilt from my constant misdeeds or impure thoughts, even though I was a good kid, I left the church as a teenager. By my twenties, I had become an obnoxious agnostic, still asking the same questions of anyone who dared express their faith around me.

Years later, I began to doubt my doubt when a class, in the anatomy and physiology of the human eye, convinced me that this body is too marvelous to have evolved by chance. This realization, coupled with an uneasy feeling that grew into unrest and then emptiness, convinced me something was missing from my existence. There had to be more to life than what I was experiencing. I then began my quest for that 'something more'.

The Path of God

A friend suggested I try Unity[1]. The new teachings at first seemed foreign to me, but the basic premise of an all-knowing, everywhere-present, the only-power-in-the-universe God appealed to me. I was attending a small Unity Church in a converted house in Modesto, California in October 1980, when a guest speaker, Reverend Carol Ruth Knox, gave the Sunday lesson. For the first time in my life, I heard a message that I knew at the core of my being was truth in large letters, all caps, bolded, and italicized. Also, have you ever had the experience of being in a crowd and making eye contact with someone and there is instant recognition, "Oh, there you are. I've been looking all over for you."? There were perhaps 125 people in the room and Carol Ruth and I connected. We talked for a bit after the service, and I knew this was a person with a special message.

---

[1] Unity is a worldwide organization regarding the life of Jesus as the premier example of how to live. It interprets the Bible metaphysically and teaches that God is within every person. (Ed.)

Introduction

'Coincidentally'[2], a few months after that first meeting, I bought a small business in Walnut Creek, California, down the street from Carol Ruth's church[3]. Over the next few years, we became dear friends and I served on her center's board of directors. We were both baseball fans and often attended games together. I rooted for the Oakland A's and she was a diehard Boston Red Sox fan. But even more than our friendship, her teachings on 'Non-duality', 'Progressing Spiritually from Victim to Victor to Vehicle', and 'The Dark Night of the Soul' changed my life and the way that I see God.

In 1985 I entered a graduate program at U.C. Santa Barbara to get an advance degree in diplomatic history. In 1987 Carol Ruth Knox was killed by an intruder. I vowed then to make Carol Ruth's lessons, which had such a profound effect on my life, available to others. I, meanwhile,

---

[2] When I say 'coincidentally' I don't mean 'coincidentally'. When suggesting that you stay consciously present in your life, one thing to watch is the so-called coincidences. I have been able to see how these instances are often connected into a pattern of one setting the stage for the next. (Ed.)

[3] Carol Ruth Knox was minister at Unity of Walnut Creek. (Ed.)

finished graduate school and went to work for the U.S. Air Force as a historian. I gathered recordings of Carol Ruth's talks, a few video tapes, and everything I could find that she had written. But I delayed editing her materials or writing on her teachings because the dichotomy between focusing upon military operations during the day and spiritual lessons at night seemed too great. I determined then I would write about Carol Ruth after I retired from the Air Force.

In 2007 I retired and began writing a book describing Carol Ruth's teachings and how they affected my life. Two years later my wife, also named Carol, was diagnosed with ovarian cancer. I realized this was a test of the teachings I had believed for more than 25 years. The book's focus shifted to applying Carol Ruth's lessons while dealing with my wife's cancer. The outcome of applying her teachings to the challenges in my life was published in 2012 as *The Dhance: A Caregiver's Search for Meaning*[4].

---

[4] Coy F. Cross II, *The Dhance: A Caregiver's Search For Meaning* (Clackamas OR: Koho Pono Publishing, 2012). See thedhance.com to order. (Ed.)

Introduction

In 2013 Unity of Walnut Creek granted me the license to publish all of Carol Ruth Knox's material. This is a 26-year-dream-come-true for me.

NOTE: *<u>The Path of God</u> is the first of Carol Ruth Knox's writings that I have edited for publication. The numbered chapters in this book are a series of talks that she gave sequentially as Sunday sermons at Unity of Walnut Creek. In addition to editing, I have added commentary and footnotes to clarify or enhance Carol Ruth's original material. My notes and commentary will be indicated with the notation (Ed.).*

- Coy F. Cross II, Ph.D.

The Path of God

1: THE PATH OF GOD

January 5, 1986

The Rarity—God

Do you realize how lucky you are to have the opportunity to spend one precious hour, once a week, to honor and to remember that God is alive? Have you remembered recently that God is working here? Have you paid any attention? Have you felt anything stir? Do you know what a stir feels like? It is a sound that vibrates inside and says, "God is working here and now." It is an opportunity to honor the fact that God is really around and doing what God is supposed to do, which is live you, cause you to become, expand you, brighten you, and give you an opportunity to remember again and again that God is indeed around. Pay attention! Wake up! This is what your life is about. Do you know this is what your life is about?

When your mate comes home and says, "I am not staying here anymore," or when the job is over, when the money isn't coming in, when you are going through the mid-life crisis, when you feel like everything is shattering and you cannot hold it together, is there a response inside that says, "God is really working now"? I want that response! I want people around me who, when they come in and say, "God, it all fell apart," so I can say, "Good, God is cooking."

God is awfully precious. You are so lucky to have the opportunity to spend an hour a week remembering so that it might infiltrate every part of your existence, so that you might feel it living in your blood. Do you know that in Judaism, only once a year are the people given the opportunity to hear the word "God"? Only once a year! Why is that done in that manner? ...So that they might cherish it. How would you feel if you had to wait one whole year to hear that word? And nobody else could say it; not you, only the Rabbi! Might you appreciate it a little bit more? Can I wake you up? Say it. Say it. Say it inside for just a minute. Say, "God." Don't let my power overwhelm you and get all shy inside; just meet me; meet me out here. If it causes a few tears, for God's sake, dare to meet it inside you and let the tears express the intimacy. Then put your whole life, all its experiences and issues into the cusp of this, the shell of this Essence, and say it again inside, "God."

Chapter 1: The Path of God

Do you know what Sunday morning services are supposed to be about? They are supposed to be about people having a rich, special opportunity of joining together, of being able to feel again something pulsate that says that they heard the Word. Sunday morning services are not about watching Carol Ruth Knox "do her thing again". They are not about personalities. This is not an entertainment festival. This is an Honor to remember to hear the Sound; to experience God! Do you understand me? I invite you to respond to this Presence. Let's not forget that the business of this church is not to be social and not to make money; it is for us to come together, to meet, and to somehow cause a vibration that will pulse inside us and cause us to go through those doors and express through our eyes and our mouths, the inner light that penetrates out from us; that we are awakened to the Existence of God. Let's remember that we are here to profess that we understand that life is not about relationships (although those may be very important); it is not about money (although it may be very important); it is not about dying (although it may be very important); it isn't about losing (although it may be very important). Life is about this analogy: in every symphony orchestra or jazz group, in the background, is a big bass viol, the one that is held upstanding; when it is played, a great bow is drawn across its strings conveying a strong, bass background, ongoing, penetrating sound. With the bass viol as the background, the rest of the orchestra plays quickly, moving flute songs, blatant trumpet calls, and mellifluous violin melodies. The fascination is that many of us call all of that surface material, 'life'. But you know what? Life's power and depth is the bass in the background—God—penetrating, sounding, and supporting it all.

What God Is

To explain God, I will only need a few paragraphs of this material. The reason I can explain God in such a small space or less is that I got very smart a few years ago when I recognized that no one can explain what God is, because there is nothing that God is not. So why describe? Most of us say that God is Love, God is Life, and God is Light. Then we all look at our dark lives and say that "God isn't there". We look at all the difficult children in our lives and say, "Well, God isn't there, I have to go find God." So let's blow the myth. Are you ready? God is not here or there, "God is". And I will lay my whole life on the line for that. Incidentally, I would like to make a general statement: I am not here to have you agree or disagree with me. Why? ...And I am going to take that one step further because what is being stated is that 'I am right for me'. If you disagree with me, you are using me as a way to discover your own truths. Through that process, you may throw me out, and I would love for you to throw me out, because then I will know that you have found YOU in relationship to God. So all you have to do is agree or disagree with *you*. But do not argue with me; it is a silly waste of time because I will throw you back on you.

God is the very life that is moving in the veins, inside, within, in the empty space, in the marrow, between the bones. Do you feel that?

God is the seeing that sees through you right now. God is the seeing.

God is the skin that is growing over the bones of your body.

God is the thread in these clothes.

God is the leaf on those plants.

God is the hair that is growing out through your eyebrows, pushing itself out through you relentlessly.

God is the confusion driving you crazy.

The Path of God

God is the question and the answer.

God is the love and the hate.

God is the newborn child and the aging-too-quickly parent.

God is two people coming together giving birth to a new one.

God is the energy in the seed that is placed in the womb.

God is the last breath that goes when death comes.

GOD IS THE WHOLE THING

Don't dare to take God out of any part of God's Universe.

One final part of this non-definition defining God. There is a tendency in many of us to say, "Well, I am not sure that God created this part of my life." I don't know, finally, how any of us could be that presumptuous to assume that there is anything that God could not create. That is ego—ego is not shining in your own light; ego is presuming that you are the boss.

Chapter 1: The Path of God

I was reading about Halley's Comet recently. While driving in Arizona a few days ago, coming out of Sedona through Oak Creek Canyon, I looked up in the sky and saw a constellation that I believe had Halley's Comet in it. I stopped, pulled over, and took-out the binoculars to look.

Halley's Comet is a fascinating story. It came into existence about fifteen billion years ago when the Earth came into form. Something happened to Halley's and we don't know what it was. (Some of us are convinced it was God, but it doesn't really matter because it is what it is.) When it came into form, this little ball of something called Halley's Comet, didn't know where it was going (kind of like you and me.) So, it got shot very fast away from the sun in a wind tunnel, spinning away out of nowhere. Maybe it looked at itself and said, "God, I wish I could get in charge of this. I wish I had a little control." Then when it got to the end of wherever it was going (which is the way it is with you and me) something went "Halt!" and Halley's Comet stayed lingering there, waiting as to whether it would go out or in. At some point in time, something said, "Come in." Ever since then it has been flying through the Universe toward the sun in 72 year patterns. I share this with you because I want to share dynamically, explicitly that the design is not yours. It is not Halley's design, it is not ours. If that is so, then the goal, the plan, is to 'put your hand in the glove'. Put your hand in the glove and let it handle your life. There is no good and bad anyway. It is just life becoming—the design is marvelous, through thick and thin, through pain and joy, through love and hate, as it destroys and creates. Its design is marvelous! The whole thing is marvelous.

The Path of God

This brings the lesson to a close. The lesson is entitled "The Path of God", not just God, but "The Path of God". There are probably four basic principles related to God—they might assist us all and give us some structure as a way to work with this marvelous force to which we give our life. I would like to make it perfectly clear right now that I do not presume that my path is any better than any others. I am just offering a path. Everybody is on a path. Khadafy[5] is on a path. And don't get all 'psyched up' that he is on a bad path. He is just on a path. Give it to him! Trust this Universal magnificence that is working in everybody to

---

[5] Carol Ruth is referring to Moammar Khadafy, the now deceased Libyan dictator. He was eventually murdered in a similar way he was known to torture opponents. (Ed.)

Chapter 1: The Path of God

unfold its mystery of becomingness, because you see, God isn't done yet. God is in everything. Please understand; please accept; please watch your inner words. When something goes wrong in your life or you see somebody who isn't acting the way you want them to act and you might say, "Ah, well, they aren't on the path." That is degrading to you and to them. If you say they are not on the path, you are playing the typical religious game of spiritual one-upmanship: since I cannot feel any better about myself any other way, I will declare myself on the path and all others who are not following the same one I follow are off! All paths are paths of God. God uses the whole thing, the whole tapestry and the threads.

Expansion: Principle One

It would appear as if we here at Unity agree about some simplistic principles about honoring the path of God and I would like to offer them to you. The first is that it would appear as if God's path involves expansion. Hear the word; take it into you. God is a God that continually expands. You may still think that God is a completion, "that in the beginning God created the heavens and the earth" and 'it' was all done, and that all we have to do is spend our lives trying to get back to God's completed perfection because we are the

The Path of God

'fallen angels'. Well, why don't you destroy that myth as well and grow with me into another, remembering that as you do, you will have to destroy it in time as well—expansion.

Let's play with a new idea to see what it does with your life; experiment with it. The image of the balloon comes from Bentov's book, *Stalking the Wild Pendulum*. There he describes God as the evolutionary theory, the big bang theory, wherein, in the beginning, the Universe expands as an expression of God, and its process is continual expansion. That happens as God continually blows his/her breath into our consciousness personally and into the whole world's consciousness so that we/it might continually evolve deeper and deeper into more expansive realms of consciousness. (That does not mean that anything that is earlier in time is less, it only means it has expanded.) As God blows his/her air into us (inspiration = blowing into), we are expanded to new extremes. Take a look at your life for a minute. Let's say your life is comfortable or uncomfortable. Let's say that somebody just came home and said, "I'm leaving." Let's say you have just lost your job. Let's say you just fell in love. Let's say you have just had the best Christmas ever. Let's say you have just had the best year financially ever. Then, again, something

Chapter 1: The Path of God

begins to move. What is happening is that God is blowing its breath into you again = inspiration. So when you start feeling life lean on you, what is happening? There is nothing wrong, you are expanding. The demand is let it do what it will. Don't try to make it go backwards, it cannot, it refuses. The greatest pain will come if you try to go back to where you were. You must let it expand. Look at your life. Look at the whole part of your life and say in one breath, "God is doing its expanding work now—I agree to participate." Say it inside, "God is breathing into me. God is breathing into me." And does that mean you are getting bigger and better? I don't know. I do know that you are expanding. I know that God is doing God's work. Put your hand in the glove. It is velvet. Please. And, the balloon of the physical universe can pop, but you as a spiritual being and principle cannot. Principle Number One: God is always expanding.

Vulnerability: Principle Two

The path of God requires vulnerability. You must become as one kneeling with arms outstretched. I cannot take this position without knowing what is required of me and being drawn to it internally. Where do we all get the myth that we are supposed to know where it is all going? Where do we all get the notion that 'it' has to be explained in English? When will we get the courage to say, "I don't know?" Very wise people say, "I don't know." I am willing to be stupid. So many miracles, so many awesome possibilities, and so many beautiful and wondrous things are denied because we are all looking for the end; we are all looking for the right information. And because we want to see the end we have our eyes focused on there, we miss all of the side and interior, and then we say, "There have been no miracles." Well, we missed them all. What is a miracle? Life is a miracle. Being here is a miracle. Isn't it wonderful—I am alive! Why must there be terms on life? Why do I have to be happy to be alive? How about just being alive? And even when you die, how about being alive with death? Principle Number Two: Vulnerability.

Art: Principle Three

The path of God requires art. Here is an example and the example teaches art. Eric Dickerson of the Los Angeles Rams ran 247 yards yesterday. A reporter was talking about Dickerson and explained that as an artistic runner he goes to the sidelines between every run and checks the taping on his ankle to be sure that it is just right for the next run. Some might call that finicky, but you know what that is? That is sensitivity, sensitivity to the whole experience that is an art. Having been a concert pianist, I know that art is a profoundly refined skill. Working with God is being sensitive: sensitive to your body, to your heart, to your mind, and to the people around you. It is molding the whole life experience so that you live the artistic dance in relationship to God. I don't know how to tell you to do it, but I know it requires the artful awareness constantly. Principle Number Three: Art.

Listening: Principle Four

This brings me to the final part of the path's requirements: listening. I was in the desert for two days this week. I had a new communion with it on this visit. In the desert, everything gets very quiet: no city lights, no cars, and no people. There is a smell that goes with it. Out there in the desert one becomes very quiet: you begin to hear – to hear at a different level. Usual thought runs on the surface like those instruments in the symphony orchestra. While out there listening, you are listening for the string bass. And how does the string bass sound? Well, it doesn't talk in words. It is a sense… something inside goes 'yes'. And how do you get to 'yes'? You listen, wait, quieter… it is not a 'yes' versus 'no', but a resounding[6] sound that confirms. Do you know what I mean? It vibrates as a response and you feel as if it all has come to move harmoniously. It isn't because the rattlesnakes went away; it isn't because there aren't any cactuses; it is because you found something beneath all that. And you did it because you took the time to listen. Listen.

Have you ever noticed that when you find special places on earth where you can listen better, you tend to make hallmarks out of them? I can tell you that my greatest weakness has been to think that I had to go to some special place to hear it. My sound is inside me, and the requirements are that I listen. And what is the call? The call is to listen deeper. And when you ask the question again, what does it say to you?

It says to you, that if you can't hear now, listen deeper.

Then when it gets all confused, and you think you have gone as far as you can and you ask, "Why is there nothing coming through?"

---

[6] Resonant and all encompassing – it can be felt inside. (Ed.)

Chapter 1: The Path of God

The Word will say, "Ask deeper."

Am I deep enough now God?

… Go deeper.

What is the call of life?

…Depth.

What is the creativity of life, where is it?

…Deep.

Will it ever end?

… No.

Would you ever want it to end?

… No… you will get awfully mad if it does. Listen. If you are in crisis, why don't you go some place where you can be quiet? Principle Number Four: Listen.

God is

God is. There is nothing else. And God's path, as I see it now, is the path of vulnerability, the path of expansion, the path of art and the path of listening. Why not take a look, experiment, and find your way of following it?

1: Carol Ruth Knox

2: THE PATH OF COURAGE

January 12, 1986

A Framework for Courage

Ten years ago my thoughts about courage were entirely different from what they are now. I was raised with a concept of faith that, "if I had the right kind of faith a certain ship would come in." So I activated faith with the hope that it would create a result. Have you ever been caught in such a concept? It worked awfully well for a long time—about thirty-eight years. And then I felt as if I lost my ability to enact faith in this manner. I had been accustomed to doing my prayer work and creating results, and if anybody said, "what is going on in your life?" or if I was struggling or having problems, I would say, "I have faith that my good will come out of this." This led to my having to cope with the issue that my good did not always come in; no matter how I manipulated my head, it didn't come out. I wanted to throw some eggs and kick some Bibles. I became angry and despairing.

The Path of God

After a period of about three or four years of this discomfort, I discovered a new word, 'courage'. Courage comes from *le coeur* meaning 'the heart'— *le coeur*, heart—courage. I know that there are people who feel, as they read this material, 'locked-in'. I know there are people reading this material who have been battling with issues of personality for a long time. I know there are people reading this material who have stayed in the wrong marriage for too long. I know there are people reading this material who are dying to open their mouths just once and tell somebody off. I know there are people reading this material who have some habit that is really 'getting them'. I know who you are; I don't know what you would write down on the sheet of paper that would say, "This is where I feel locked-in; this is my prison; or this is where I have wound the circle around my feet so I can't move." I don't know what yours is. I know there are people reading this material who for ten or fifteen years have been waiting to 'fly the coop'. (And I don't know what your coop is.) I know there are people reading this material who have been living a lifestyle that doesn't fit and who would give anything to breakout. I know there are people reading this material who have said a million times, "I am not going to pick up another drink of alcohol again." And yet, tomorrow, they do. Or, "I am not going to let my

Chapter 2: The Path of Courage

life be put-out by that man ever again,"—but at the next moment of encounter, they quake and quiver and shy and cop-out. I know there are men reading this material that have been castrated by women and learned to be 'dainty' around them. And yet tomorrow, they will be dainty again. Jesus says, "Don't put your light under a bushel." We hear these words and something rises up saying, "Oh, God, that's wonderful." Then at the next opportunity, we let the light go out.

So many of us live life this way, we walk up to the situation or issue gingerly, slowly, look at the cliff edge, then back-away and cower, running to the rear. Then we charge to the edge again, but we never leap—never. Our life is spent walking, running to the edge. The tragedy of life is how many of us get old too soon. We had a huge circle when we were born. (I don't think it[7] is a straight line; it is a circle.) Each moment of our life when somebody said, "No," or some gesture said, "Uh, uh," or some verb said "Don't,"...

We said, "Okay, okay, okay... okay... okay."

---

[7] It = life. (Ed.)

Now, if we don't want to let these recognitions cause us to feel sorry for ourselves; if we want to find a way to poke our finger through the web; if we want to find a way to move out beyond the eggshell (and we all always are in an eggshell, just continually bigger ones), the key is *le coeur*—courage. It isn't a syrupy, sickening, 'Oh, I have faith in God'. Some churches teach that kind of approach and I can smell it a mile away. But courage is a solid, confirmed conviction contained within one's being based on trust in the Presence that is God functioning always, everywhere, needing no proof, no results.

Kierkegaard's Dancer

In Soren Kierkegaard's book, <u>Fear and Trembling and the Sickness unto Death</u>, he describes courage. When I discovered these words, in 1978, I was beginning to walk down here on earth… I had taken away the covers[8]. I had dealt with my psychological self and now I was approaching my spiritual self. I was shaking. I was in dread, I was in despair, and I wore both. I didn't know how to cope, I didn't know what to do next, and in that state I was given the awareness of courage: "It is

---

[8] The stories or practices that she believed kept her safe. (Ed.)

Chapter 2: The Path of Courage

supposed to be the most difficult task for a dancer[9] to leap into a definite posture in such a way that there is not a second when he is grasping after the posture, but by the leap itself he (or she) stands fixed in that posture."[10]

You see, the problem with most of our living is that we imagine, we grasp after, and we never leap. The people enclosed in the circle are the ones who did not leap. We use the phrase "Go for it" a lot in our society. The problem with the "Go for it" phrase is that we assumed we knew where we would land. One does not live courageously if he/she has to know whether the earth will reach out and grab you or how you will land or who will catch you. You just must leap and spend your life in the instant of leaping. Kierkegaard goes on to say,

> *Perhaps no dancer can do it--[these people are the 'dancers of life'. It deserves the eloquent, it deserves the sophisticated.] Perhaps no dancer can do it—that is what this knight of courage does. Most people live dejectedly in*

---

[9] "Dancer": when Carol Ruth Knox pronounced the word in her Bostonian accent, it sounded like dhancer ("a" pronounced like "ah"). (Ed.)

[10] Soren Kierkegaard, *Fear and Trembling*, p. 51

> *worldly sorrow and joy; they are the ones who sit along the wall and do not join in the dance. The knights of infinity are dancers and possess elevation. They make the movements upward, and fall down again; and this too is no mean pastime, nor ungraceful to behold. But whenever they fall down and are not able at once to assume the posture, they vacillate in an instant and this vacillation shows that after all they are strangers in the world.*[11]

That is probably the most important statement Kierkegaard has to say in this passage. You see, most of us have wanted to be able to leap in life; and when we fall and crumble-up, and have nobody see us, we say, "Oh, I'm okay—I'm fine." We are afraid to share with the whole world that we are vulnerable, that we are crying, that it isn't okay here, but even in the not-okay-ness we are dancers—elevated. Do you feel that? Then vulnerability too becomes a courageous act. The present movies *Rocky* and *Rambo* are stories of the one who always wins in the end, the Hollywood ending. Fully mesmerized by this hope, we always want the winner out there. What we need are some new scripts that show the beauty of the one who fell when they leapt, so that we can all feel

---

[11] Soren Kierkegaard, *Fear and Trembling*, p. 52

equally wonderful about falling or rising. That is courage. Don't you like it? Doesn't it feel right?

Three Qualities in the Dancer

I: You've Gotta Go

There appear to be three simple qualities evident in the dancer, and if we observe them, then we might live them. First, if you are going to live the courageous life, you must function with this feeling, "you've just 'gotta' go." You've just gotta go. And if you don't know what you are going for, you just still must go. I went down to my boat yesterday morning, and I sat in the fog. I had taken my boat out in the fog once, and as soon as I got out of the harbor, I turned right around and brought it back in. I got off the boat after doing some studying and reading. As I left the boat and noticed there was a boat coming into the harbor, I was really impressed. The men piloting the boat we might call, 'rednecks'—fisherman type, hunters. I went up to them and said, "Do you take your boat out in the fog? How do you do that?"

And they said, "Oh, yes, you can take your boat out in the fog." And they said simply, "You've just gotta go. Sometimes we don't make it. We almost hit the Antioch Bridge the other day."

The Path of God

That's the point—they go whether they make it or not! Of course, they use a compass, but you have to be careful when you hear this kind of teaching that you don't over scrutinize what is said. This is a Principle – a posture – a movement about being courageous. The doing is not important, nor the how—live with the feeling of courage in you and let it move you. You don't have to figure out whether Carol Ruth Knox should take her boat out in the fog (and I did not yesterday), but rather, get the point. You've just got to go.

Let me show you something on the piano to bring this home. [At this point, Dr. Knox[12] plays a Chopin Polonaise. In one section she has to leave the keys to touch the keys at opposite ends of the keyboard, unable to see where her hands will land. She demonstrates two ways—one, not leaping and checking everything out first and then leaping without concern for the landing.] The point obviously is that as long as one checks everything out and never leaps, you can never get the feeling of the 'thing'—of life, of the experience, etc. This

---

[12] Carol Ruth Knox received a Master's Degree in Musicology from Brown University and a Ph.D. from the California Institute of Integral Studies-San Francisco. She was a highly accomplished musician in addition to her many other gifts. (Ed.)

Chapter 2: The Path of Courage

example is an attempt to show that I am willing to take the leap of courage whether I make it or not... I have to go!

My teacher had to work with me to do this—one day I was sitting struggling through this trying, making limited gestures and movements when Charles Moulton[13] said, "C'mon Carol, this time—just do it!" So, I did.

At this point, many people stand around saying, "Well, when I'm ready." I have hated that line all my life! Don't you ever get tired of it? It is the spiritual cop-out—our most recent one[14]. We got too smart to say, "Well, I'm too old or too young" or "I'm not good enough." We now say, "I'm not quite ready." You are always ready and you are never ready. Readiness is a point in the infinite that one keeps moving through and through— you just GO! Cut out talking about it.

Here is a wonderful story about a man in Montreal:

---

[13] Charles Moulton was Carol Ruth's music teacher. (Ed.)

[14] Recent in humankind's spiritual evolution (Ed.)

The Path of God

Employees were having a hard time adjusting to working in Montreal's new skyscrapers. In one lofty office, secretaries, afraid they might trip and crash through the glass, refused to walk near the windows. Company officials called in an engineer to solve the problem. He removed his safety hat, walked to one end of the office, wheeled about, ran back the length of the office and hurled his 200-pound frame against the window. He bounced back with a thud, retrieved his hat and silently returned to his duties in the basement.

I have never told this story before, but when I came out here fifteen years ago to become the minister at this Center, I was thirty-one years old. As I prepared, I was shocked at what happened to me. I had a little apartment in Lee's Summit, Missouri. When I came back from visiting my home, I realized I was heading another 1,500 miles west, now 3,000 miles away from everybody that I knew, everybody who loved me, and every being, every form, and every shape that was familiar. I felt myself deeply burdened by something that wouldn't let me move. I was supposed to be having my whole house packed and found myself lying on the couch. I had never experienced anything like that before. I couldn't move. I guess you could say that I was really depressed or lonely or lost. Yet, at some point, something inside finally said, "Go." And I did.

Chapter 2: The Path of Courage

Probably the most courageous act I have ever done concerning 'Go' happened to me at Masada, Israel. Masada is a flat mound high up in the air; it is the place where the Jews defended themselves against the Romans back in 79 A.D. When one gets up on top of Masada, he/she can see the whole Dead Sea area. I felt a profound basic fear; a feeling that when I get up on heights, I want to challenge them; I wanted to run off the edge of Masada into the Dead Sea. And to this day, I don't know how I didn't. The message then was not "go", it was "stop"... the GO then was STOP. Somehow I seemed to obey that, but then the most courageous thing I had to do was to walk down the steps, off that huge cliff. The only way I could get down was to sit down each step. But I did it. The dancer leaps.

II: Without Thinking

Second, it must be done without thinking. Yesterday a plane crashed in San Jose. A man went into the plane and pulled out the pilot who was in flames. He described how he was able to do it: "Without thinking, I crashed through the door of the airplane and pulled him out." And today that man is a hero. This lesson is talking about heroic living. And you know: I am not talking to a group of people who are dire or down-and-out. I am talking to a group of people who are the 'cream', that is who I talk to every Sunday morning—the cream. Sometimes those who are the cream can rest easier on their laurels because they don't have crises to draw forth their heroic selves. It is really easy to be courageous in a crisis. Being courageous moment-to-moment is letting each moment of your life be the leap—the courageous leap, in the instant, falling or rising—that is courageous when you are the 'cream'. I am talking about heroic, moment-to-moment leaping/living—without thinking.

Now, does that mean that when you face a challenge or an issue that you don't think? No, of course not! Don't be preposterous with my words. Without thinking means only that in that moment when you take the leap, you cannot, you must not think! I watched my brother working upstairs in my attic (which is being redesigned). I was with him Thursday, assisting him. There was a beam that was sitting higher up in the middle of the floor; it was sitting up just a quarter of an inch too high above the rest of the floor. The beam that was sitting higher was a major beam of the house. There was only one thing to do... cut a quarter of an inch off it using a skill saw. Well, those of you who work with skill saws know what is being described here. What has to be done is to

Chapter 2: The Path of Courage

lie down on the floor and run the skill saw a quarter of an inch across the wood. Well, I watched him. He measured; we worked with the level this way and that way; then he took a chalk line and placed it along the wood that had to be cut. I watched him walk around it; he thought it through; and he thought some more. And then all of a sudden, he went and picked up the skill saw, lay down on the floor and started the cut. You see, the final act had to be without thought.

We here at the Center have done something without thought. We don't talk about it too much as we are kind of plodding along with it right now. We bought land about six months ago. When we bought that land, what did we have to do? We had to throw all reason to the wind. It doesn't make sense that this Center should be able to build a two-million-dollar complex. It doesn't look as if we have the people-power or the money-power. Yet, we had been pushed to our limits in this space and we had sat here for eight years, waiting—thinking—figuring. Then one day, in a board meeting, with a lot of fear, and with a lot of resistance, a group said, "Now." Without thinking, Action[15], very often, doesn't make sense.

III: Renunciation

In order to move courageously, one must also renounce all. I would like to read to you Luke 14:26:

> *If any one comes to me and does not hate his own father and mother and wife and children and brothers and sisters, yes, and even his own life, he cannot be my disciple.*

Can you hear that in terms of courage? "If anybody comes to me and doesn't hate his own father, mother, wife, children, brother, sister, yes, even his own life, he cannot be my disciple." Jesus is talking about courage. He is saying you have to hate everything that is around you (and this is not revengeful hate—this is like saying, "I must renounce everything in order to go"), in order to move—leap—act.

You can't sit around saying, "Maybe if I do this, this is right," or, "Well, if I stop smoking then I'll

---

[15] Action is deliberately capitalized to represent divine action as a decision. This will be a convention for similar words throughout the book. (Ed.)

Chapter 2: The Path of Courage

feel like this," or, "If I start drinking, I'll feel like that." It has to be that you must hate all reason, all everything else, and MOVE, that is what Jesus is talking about. [16]

Isak Dinesen, in the story of her life, says it this way:

> *The essence of all great gestures is to mock necessity, economic, biological or narrative. The gesture does not defy the bourgeoisie impulse to appraise and experience in practical terms, in terms of its market value. One is forced by life to pay the price for one's existence. And this is pain, loss and death. One is also free to laugh at the price and at one's self for caring about it. The essence of all great gestures is to mock necessity.*[17]

And what we usually pay attention to is: necessity; the terms; the situations; and what will I do and what will I use? The act of courage—just move, without thought, without expectation NOW—now—now—and again—and again—NOW.

---

[16] It is an act of commitment, certainty and priority without reservation. In *The Bible* by George Lamsa, the word "hate" is translated from the Aramaic as "put aside". (Ed.)

[17] Isak Dinesen, *Out of Africa*, p. 248

Another example of this same point is seen in the story of Antoinette Bourignon, the spiritual leader who made such a stir in the religious world of the seventeenth century. As a young girl, she had a great vision of her spiritual unity with God, coupled with a great desire to communicate to the people of her day who were walking in such great darkness. Her parents were on the verge of forcing her into an unwelcome marriage, so she decided to leave home. One morning, at daybreak, she started on her way, taking with her one penny for bread for that day. As she was leaving the house, she felt a presence within her saying, "Where is your faith, in a penny?"

Without a moment's hesitation, she threw the penny aside and replied, "No, Lord, my faith is in Thee and in Thee alone."

Courage Is God

And finally, the question must be answered, if you are going to leap, why bother? What is going to catch you? I would like to have you imagine something that I really know awfully well, an image which will assist you. Maybe it is something you can carry with you for the rest of your life. Can you imagine that out there, over the ledge of your experience, there are a group of balloons

Chapter 2: The Path of Courage

with strings? The group of balloons with strings is analogous to the Principle of the Universe. This Principle of the Universe is, if you leap, God will catch you. Because just as all gravity is pulling most of us down, I can assure you that God is also there, pulling you up. Do you feel that? Do you know it? [Even at the time of death, God is there to catch you. (Ed.)]

> *I am standing on the seashore. A ship at my side spreads her white sails to the morning breeze and starts for the blue ocean. She is an object of beauty and strength, and I stand and watch her until at length she is a speck of white cloud just where the sea and sky come to mingle with each other. Then someone at my side says, 'There! She's gone!' Gone where? Gone from my sight, that is all. She is just as large in mast and hull and spar as she was when she left my side, and she is just as able to bear her load of living weight to her destined harbor. Her diminished size is in me, not in her. And just at the moment when someone at my side says, 'There! She's gone!' there are other eyes watching her coming, and other voices ready to take up the glad shout, 'There she comes!' And that is dying. – Anonymous*

The only way that you can find this out is to leap. You must understand that the Principle of God is an ascending Principle. It is leaven. Leaven is that stuff inside you that rises. You don't have to make yourself rise. You do have to reach out and grab the balloon string. Something there will catch you.

The Path of God

The reason that the dancer can leap is because the dancer knows that the dancer will be caught, whether the dancer rises or falls.

In closing, I would like to share this poem by Rainer Maria Rilke:

> *The leaves are falling, falling as if from far up, as if orchards were dying high in space.*
>
> *Each leaf falls as if it were motioning "NO!"*
>
> *And tonight the heavy earth is falling away from all the other stars in the loneliness.*
>
> *We are all falling. This hand here is falling. And look at the other one. It's in them all.*
>
> *And yet there is Someone, whose hands infinitely calm, holding up all this falling.*[18]

---

[18] *Selected Poems of Rainer Maria Rilke*, trans. Robert Bly, (New York: Harper and Row, Publishers Inc. 1981) p. 89

3: THE PATH OF EVOLUTION

January 19, 1986

Evolution Defined

An atomic blast reduced the earth to a mass of rubble. The last survivor, an ape, emerged from a cave, rubbing his eyes and looked around. A few days later a female ape emerged from another cave. "Say, do you have anything to eat?" asked the male ape. Without saying a word, the female returned to her cave and came out with an apple. The male took one look at it. "Oh, no," he exclaimed, "You're not going to start that all over again."

We are all on the path of evolution whether we would like to be or not. I would go so far, and be so bold, as to say that those who don't even believe they are on the path of evolution are screening themselves from the truth that one day we will all believe and accept. When I use the word evolution, I am not referring necessarily to the issue that has caused such a concern in the public school systems, i.e., whether we come from the apes. I do not have any problem with the fact that maybe I came from an ape. I do know that when my consciousness (our consciousness, universally, as a group of humans) came into existence at that moment in time there was what is called 'the hundredth monkey experience'[19]. In other words, we were all rolling around at our level of consciousness and at a significant point of expansion there was a huge POP and consciousness was shifted dramatically—probably in an instant—into what is now called human consciousness. That occurrence was the activity of God working; evolution does not remove God from God's Universe. Rather, the evolutionist's theory really pushes God so far into the whole creative manifestation that it is impossible to remove God from it.

In sharing these ideas on evolution, my hope is that you will complete reading this material and gain a deep feeling of how much you are being promulgated, pushed, created, moved, shaped, molded, and expanded, truly and entirely, by the act of God—and there is no way that you can

---

[19] 'The hundredth monkey' is a term made popular by Ken Keyes in his book, *The Hundredth Monkey*. The effect is defined as the rapid spread of a powerful new idea in a population once a critical mass of acceptance is reached. Some believe that the propagation of ideas occurs through a phenomenon of non-locality. (Ed.)

Chapter 3: The Path of Evolution

remove any aspect of your life from that activity of God. In this total view, even that choice where you think you made up your mind isn't really your choice, but is instead a choice that has moved through you by the evolutionary activity of God who always has in God's mind the interest, of the whole, of you, and of the race, in Its mind. Is that clear? Feel inside of your life.

It is so common with human beings to look at life and presume that whatever is happening is our fault. Suppose I were to announce to the whole world that it is not your fault. How would you feel about it? Might you feel a bit lighter and maybe a little bit scared because you no longer have any control? If you keep thinking that it is your fault, then your ego becomes involved, and you can take credit for it. If you give it up and say that it is not your fault, you are not an issue. This is God unfolding, unraveling God's mystery, like a great tapestry through each of us—then you cannot take credit for it either. The ego has to get out of the way totally. Then that word 'vehicle' becomes strikingly important: I am here to be used, to be an instrument for God... to be played through. I find that exciting. I find that relieving. I find that freeing. I find that does not need scrutinizing. It does not need my mind then. The fear about this kind of teaching, however, is that it is assumed that if human beings are let loose they will burn each other, butcher each other, and desecrate each other, etc. My inclination, however, is to assume that if human beings are let loose, they will be more available to love. And the love they will express is not romantic love alone, but rather a love power that is pulling on this whole Universe. That Love power is God. The whole thing is God anyway, but there is a Love power that is pulling at us.

Push-Pull

To explain this more completely, would you imagine with me for a moment a diamond shape. Through this image can be seen how the evolutionary process works. Imagine the tip of the diamond being a pulling power and the bottom tip being a pushing power. At the top of the diamond is the activity of Love, God, caressing, shaping, molding, and pulling on the individual and the whole. As it pulls, so at the bottom is that same power, God, Love, caressing, shaping, and molding by pushing up on the individual and Universal consciousness. As I look at this, I see a push-pull dynamic—isn't it interesting that we think of pushing and pulling as antagonistic, opposite, whereas in this image, it is moving together evolutionarily. What if the process is

Chapter 3: The Path of Evolution

you—you are being pushed and pulled by the activity of God? And when you feel inside a certain kind of pain or a certain kind of darkness or a certain kind of fog, it isn't that something is out of order, but rather, something is happening.

Tielhard de Chardin describes this pull as the Noosphere. Chardin, a Jesuit priest, who had studied biology most of his life, and whose works were hidden from the Roman Catholic church because they were not accepted and were not released until after his death, describes what is going on in the Universe as this Noosphere: something mighty powerful is pulling on us— always has been pulling us toward an Omega Point. And the Omega Point itself is always expanding. The Omega Point isn't an ending, it is always an opening—an opening—an opening. It is happening in you.

Consider this quotation from Romain Gary[20]:

I see history as a relay race in which each one of us, before dropping in his tracks, must carry one stage further the challenge of being a person. I refuse to find anything final in our biological, intellectual or physical limitations. My hope

---

[20] A French Novelist and Diplomat of the 20th century (Ed.)

> *knows no frontiers. So confident am I of the outcome of the struggle, whether personal or international, that sometimes I experience a gaiety, an intoxication of hope, a certainty of victory so intense that on our age-old battlefield covered with rusty shields and broken swords and atom bombs, I still feel as if I was standing on the eve of our first fight. A spark of confidence of gaiety keeps going in me and only needs a darkening shadow around me to blow it into a triumphant flame. Human stupidity may make the angels weep, but it always seems to me that people are never more clearly its victims than when they are His instruments.*

That is an affirmation of the whole process, the whole thing is unfolding.

Such a teaching will test you to the core because you will have to look at everything in the light of this. You will have to look at rape; you will have to look at war; you will have to look at the famine in Africa; you will have to look at the closest person and thing and experience in your life and say, "And this too—and this too. But can't I exclude this one? My anger, can't I exclude it; the unkindness—it doesn't fit, nor this or this—those don't fit." And I'll bet sometimes you use me by hearing inside, "Carol, but not this one."

And you can be sure you will hear my echo saying, "Yes, this one, too and this one, too. Get your

Chapter 3: The Path of Evolution

mind out of the way; give it over, trust, trust, and trust."

Trust my pain?

Yes, trust it.

Trust my anger because I was mistreated?

Yes, trust your anger.

Trust my confusion?

Yes, trust your confusion.

Trust this love?

Yes

… and this joy, this hunger, this desire?

Yes.

Trust this emptiness, this void, this pathetic hollow, my inadequacy, and my insecurity?

Yes, trust it.

You mean that's God?

Yes, that's God—that's God—that's God. You cannot remove God from God's Universe, friends. I won't let you. And capturing such an idea, does that give you some infinitesimal hope? ...Bigger than the hope that it will all turn out good, according to your conditioned mind?

Tell me, does it? Isn't it a buoyant awareness that lifts you above it all?

Creativity as Expansion

Let's review the idea on creation as presented in the first lesson of this series. God is primarily an evolutionary activity. Some beliefs hold that the Universe and you and all consciousness was designed, in the beginning, as a completed composite. Then you and I fell out of its perfection state, which God has created and became sinners or lost souls. Then, poetically, a ladder was built in our minds whereby we could spend the rest of our lives climbing up that ladder, trying to get back inside, trying to get back to perfection. Obviously, that is a very difficult life style, spending the rest of your life trying to get back to perfection. Then you are not only working, but you are 'working to get to heaven'. There is another theory, prescribed by Itzhak Bentov, based upon New Physics and found in

Chapter 3: The Path of Evolution

Stalking the Wild Pendulum. He describes simply that Creation is a process of ongoing expansion. Nothing is complete in the beginning; perfection is the continual, ongoing state of becoming as all life expands. That which is as it becomes is perfection. That is the Greek meaning for the word perfection: as you are now is perfection. It is not something you go back to; it is not something you try to get to; it is something that is becoming, always, now.

Bentov goes on to describe how the Universe works using a balloon as an analogy. Imagine that blowing the air into the balloon is the activity of God continually breathing God's breath into the Universe, i.e. God breathes God's breath into your husband's consciousness, into the race consciousness, into the Russian consciousness, again into the race consciousness, into the South African's consciousness, and into the Afghani's consciousness—always breathing God's breath. The word 'inspiration' is a wonderful word. Inspiration simply means from the Latin: 'Spiro' = 'I breathe'; 'in' = 'into'; 'tion' = 'the state of breathing the breath into'. Our attitude toward inspiration has been that it 'dropped-in' from somewhere if we were in a 'right' state of mind, with its power leading us to feel good. We have had little sense that maybe inspiration is always working even at that point of greatest discomfort. Based upon this image, as the breath blows in, we are being inspired, we are being stretched.

Now, let's look at how this works literally. You are 'hanging around' and you begin to feel uncomfortable. What is happening? You are being pushed up against the interior edge of the balloon. Feel that! You are being pushed up against the edge of the interior of that balloon. Up to this point, prior to the breath blowing in, you were feeling comfortable inside (and using another image), inside your egg. So, there you are, comfortable and all of a sudden, or gradually, the breath is blown in and you start getting pushed up against the interior wall of the egg. That may show as depression. (How do you feel that pressure inside you? What are you experiencing when you start feeling pushed up against the interior edge of the present egg? How does that express inside you?) Heavy? Hopeless? Tired? Disoriented? Panicked? Frustrated? Angry? Impatient? Confused?[21] Our words might be, "I just thought I had it made. I thought I just got this relationship right. I thought I just got this job

---

[21] All emotions and feelings are indicators of the inspiration and expansion of God working in and through you. (Ed.)

Chapter 3: The Path of Evolution

down pat. And, then, the great breath enters into my consciousness." Just understand it—just accept it for what it is.

And when the pressure starts pushing on you, stop trying to get back to where you were, and allow yourself be pressed on through the webbing of the eggshell inside, to poke your head out—to be born again—which is regeneration, which is resurrection—all done inside this physical lifetime. And when you poke yourself out what will you find? You will begin to feel comfortable with what you have become, because the unknown will have passed and you can start breathing easily. But you will find that if you continue expanding (and you will always continue expanding), just as you begin to feel comfortable, you will look up and see the edge of the interior of another egg. And then the great breath will enter again. In line with this, it is so exciting to me to observe that most of us experience pain when we have already grown internally beyond the present state. In other words, usually, at the point at which we feel pain, it is because we have already grown internally beyond our present state and are feeling the frustration of being let out beyond the limits which we can no longer stand. We have grown too big for the present egg. The point of discomfort is that we are already too big for the present egg. Trust that. Trust that.

Em<u>urge</u>ncy[22]

Evolution feels like the pushing of a banana through its skin to protrude the banana fruit forward and let go of the skin that falls by the side. Evolution feels urgent—I want you to feel urgent—it is the inner urge—urge—em<u>urge</u> [purposely misspelled]. And when the egg begins to shatter, when the habit begins to be so obvious you cannot ignore it anymore, when the discomfort of the job can no longer be acceptable—then the em<u>urging</u>, the inspiration is pushing you beyond who you were, and you have already arrived where you were intended to become—once the shells around you are broken and you are fully living where you are intended to be, then the discomfort will pass. When who we have become is too big for whom we were; or when who we are is too small for our sense of being, then we are in a state of em<u>urge</u>ncy. If you can accept this sense of self, do you realize how much easier your life is going to be? Do you realize how much you are going to be able to just

---

[22] Emerge + urgency = Emurgency

enjoy being shattered and broken and molded and shaped and changed? I do. Don't call it masochistic! Let's change those words all around. I hope evolution feels clear, like you are a part of it, so that you can cooperate with it—get into it!

The Process of Evolution

Let's address this process of evolution through the first three verses of Genesis.

> *In the beginning God created the heavens and the earth. The earth was without form and void, and darkness was upon the face of the deep. And the Spirit of God was moving over the face of the waters. Genesis 1: 1-3*

Feel that image! "Darkness was upon the face of the deep." Don't you feel dark sometimes? I am sure you do. The Bible continues on in this state boldly saying, "And the Spirit of God was moving over the face of the waters." What trust! What trust! What have most of us done with our darkness, with our evolutionary process? We have said that we will do anything to get out of the darkness—anything. I will run away, I will drink more, I will leave this relationship. None of those activities are wrong, but we have not trusted that the Spirit of God was moving upon the face of the water. In last week's lesson, I asked you to grab a hold of the balloon strings to put your trust in the bounty supporting you—that is God's Spirit moving on the face of the waters while there is darkness on the face of the deep. And then, out of all this, the passage states, "God said, 'Let there be light'."

In the beginning God created...

So many of us, we want everything to come to a clearly defined end. So many of us want to be sure of the result—the product. So many of us want to get married and have it all taken care of on that day for the next fifty years. So many of us hate beginnings, yet this passage recognizes every instant is a beginning. And the freshest roses on the face of the earth are the ones who are continually willing to be the beginning, as it is. They are the ones who have life. Those are the ones who are living in the womb with the seed popping... popping... popping.

"In the beginning God created the heavens and the earth." Have you listened to these words recently—have you read these words recently? "In the beginning God created the heavens and the earth." It doesn't say that God created only the heavens. God created the earth, too. God created the bowels of the earth out of which we come. In Egypt, the scarab beetle is a symbol for the

Chapter 3: The Path of Evolution

country early in the country's history. The nature of that scarab beetle is that it pushes its own dung towards the sun. Look at the power of that image. Most of us Americans and Westerners want to get out of our dung. We don't appreciate that material must be used as the basis of our evolution. It is out of that dung that the banana penetrates through the skins into its new self. You don't ignore it, the stuff of yourself, the dung—the nature of evolution is not to just leap over itself but to work its way through the material at hand. Evolution works in a spiral. It comes back and around and pushes through and then back and around. It is a dance movement, it is a flow. No part is rejected. Aren't we learning that? We are getting away from positive thinking that says, "Throw out this because you know what is right and what is wrong." We are shouting-out to ask that everyone live-out the whole thing. Evolution works through the image of the infinity circle. It is an ancient arc—it brings one back and then pulls them forward and the movement is again that of a dance; in Hindu the dance is called Lila.[23] It says, "Come on folks, let's use all of our material; permit the use of the heavens and of the earth. Let yourself use your confusion and your anger

---

[23] It translates as "divine play". (Ed.)

and your passion and your love and your joy and your saintliness and your devil—and let it all be used to create you, because God indeed is using it all."

"In the beginning God created the heavens and the earth."

The Earth Was Without Form...

"The earth was without form and void, and darkness was upon the face of the deep." You know what that state is like, don't you? I am suggesting that we be willing to be in that state of being without form and void. I am suggesting we make that a way of living. I am suggesting that structures set you up for disappointments and letdowns and limits. Oh, we need the structure to know how to walk, how to run our business, and how to open our mouths; but in terms of the 'guts' of our beings, in terms of the internal life of ourselves, or in terms of the God of you and me and what it wants from us, it is an open human who is willing to be in the void. 'In the void' means to be open, to be willing to not know what is going on—to be available. Structure cannot be molded or bent. It can only be broken.

I am like a flag in the center of open space.

Chapter 3: The Path of Evolution

I sense ahead the wind which is coming, and must live it through, while the things of the world still do not move: the doors still close softly, and the chimneys are full of silence, the windows do not rattle yet, and the dust still lies down.

I already know the storm, and I am as troubled as the sea. I leap out, and fall back, and throw myself out, and am absolutely alone in the great storm.[24]

We want the world to give us indications that the track we are on is right. But the world doesn't move. Or it moves too slowly, have you noticed? So you have to trust the internal, the void, the emptiness—the space. "The dust still lies down." When there is movement inside you, do you want something outside to show it to you? But that is not what happens in the void. The void is full of silence and waiting and mystery. It is womb-like. Can you feel that? Can you give your lives up?[25] "I already know the storm and I am as troubled as the sea. I leap out and fall back and throw myself out and I am absolutely alone in the great storm."

---

[24] *Selected Poems of Rainer Maria Rilke*, trans. Robert Bly, (New York: Harper and Row, Publishers Inc. 1981) p. 79

[25] Can you release your expectations of a particular process or outcome? Can you just be there in the intensity of change? ...of Creation? (Ed.)

Can you imagine what the earth felt like the day it was born? It was a holocaust of fire. It was coming out of its void-ness into form. It was not very comfortable.

And darkness moved...

"And darkness moved upon the face of the deep." Feel that depth in these lines! What is this state like? It is a womb waiting to be impregnated, and I use the symbol carefully—a womb waiting to be impregnated. And the sexuality here is that the impregnation takes place through the activity of God. One does not actively seek someone else for external impregnation—no, you must wait if you want the great moment, if you want more of life in the womb of your Self, trusting that Spirit is moving across the face of the waters. I have lived a long time in that womb, I want to keep a portion of me in there always, and I think I do.[26]

If you were to ask me how I prepare these Sunday lessons, I would answer, "I hang around." I live life and I hang around. I feel like a being that has a great receptacle and watch something from life

---

[26] It is an alert waiting and active receptivity—not an action to be fulfilled through personal intent. (Ed.)

Chapter 3: The Path of Evolution

drop-in during the week and recognize that it fits. "That's it," I hear inside, and I swallow it, and then I cherish it, and it grows. Maybe one of you shares something from your life, or maybe I receive a phone call, a letter, and watch it fall into the womb, impregnating me; and I swallow it and it grows as I trust that the Spirit is moving across the face of these waters of my being.

When one first starts living like this you can expect to get awfully anxious—awfully nervous—because it is so unique, especially in Western life, to come to a stop with life. To let life feed us from the internal—the eternal—rather than the external only. It is possible. You may discover living in these deep waters becomes a way of life. That does not mean you stop externally—you don't see me stopping externally. It is an internal willingness to wait resiliently.

Let there be Light

"Let there be Light." Imagine, for a minute, a deep pool. You are a deep pool. Everyone is a deep pool. Stop living at the surface. Stop giving your authority away to everybody else to tell you who you are and what you should do next. Start remembering, that you are the Grand Canyon and you have only touched the top layer. The call of discomfort is to go deeper. In that pool, you have already covered so many layers, so many levels of it, and then the fog appears over the water. The void appears over the water. Something in you says, "I have to start moving." But it is not outward—it is inward. What happens at the moment of moving inward is that you begin to wait for the light to shine through the present surface material in to the next layer of depth that lies within you. And how will that layer of depth show itself? It does call for meditation; it does call for ongoing prayer and it calls for infinitesimally deeper and deeper listening.

What happens when you listen? How does God speak? How does God shine the light? We have assumed that God would shine the light with big bold letters. We have hoped that one of those planes flying in the sky with a streamer saying, "Jane, go here" or, "Tony, leave Matilda." No. No. God is deeply subtle. And my sense is that God's most infinitesimal subtle showing, in the pond as the light, deeper still is a feeling. And feeling is not emotion. Spiritual feelings are sensations of clarity and knowing, experienced in the body system. They sound like a friendly "yes." And when it floats into you, it feels solid and in-place. Something inside says, "Now," and one must be very alert. You must be very awake. It

Chapter 3: The Path of Evolution

may come in a dream; it may come in a meditation; it may come as you turn the corner in your car. The next level at which listening shows could be called a sense. It is not as powerful or as clear as a knowing, a spiritual feeling, but a sensation moves in the system. It may be a 'swash' of light moving inside that gives you an indication, a tone. The next level of listening shows itself as an idea. When the idea springs into the mind, you recognize it as clarity—"Yes, that's it." And the next form in which listening shows is action. Feeling—sense—idea—action.

Just a reminder—sometimes the indications in the depths of the waters are to go totally against the grain of everything you know to be right. So many talk about this part of life and their indicators being that "it was clear that this was what I should do." Sometimes God speaks by going against the grain. Don't always look for ease. Sometimes the call is to go against everything you know to be right.

To bring this to a close and support this idea of listening in depth, here is T. S. Eliot from his *Four Quartets*:

Descend lower, descend only
Into the world of perpetual solitude,
World not world, but that which is not world,

The Path of God

*Internal darkness, deprivation
And destitution of all property,
Desiccation of the world of sense,
Evacuation of the world of fancy,
Inoperancy of the world of spirit;
This is the one way, and the other
Is the same, not in movement
But abstention from movement; while the world moves
In appentency, on its mettaled ways
Of time past and time future.*

2: Carol holding Cindy on the waters

4: THE PATH OF LOVE (CHERISH)

February 2, 1986

Introduction

It is so hard to talk about love. Why? Because it is a living attitude—and you commit to it and live it. No philosophy can ultimately explain it. I made a commitment to love a long, long time ago. My first noteworthy experience took place on a football field about twenty years ago. I had been the band director, who had stood up and played the *Star Spangled Banner*, while there was a melee on the football field. As I walked off the field someone from the opposing side was so angry because I had brought the fight to a halt through playing the *Star Spangled Banner* that he struck me on my face. I was already committed to love. There was nothing to do except to love; there was no reason to fight back. I have told you recently about being in Egypt and taking a picture of a young child, which was against their culture. The father was enraged at me and slapped me. Again, my commitment to love stopped overt reaction—that commitment to love inside was far too deep.

The Path of God

Although I consider that my life has been easy, if I were to tell you some of the 'rotten' parts of my life, you might say that my life has not been easy. I have been mistreated by people who have loved me—haven't you? I have walked through some pretty shoddy spaces trying to prove that I am 'loving'. I have let myself be treated in some pretty awful ways by the people who profess their love of me. But, regardless, I am proud of the reality that there isn't a person on the face of the earth with whom I have had a relationship, that I can't go up to and greet with my heart open and say, "I love you." Somewhere in me, I never wanted to close down. I never wanted to shut-off. Do you know about that? And do you know about being shut-off? And do you know about hardening your heart? Do you know about closing-down? And finally, do you know how difficult that is on anyone? Having shared this preface—concerning the necessary action of love—let me share the only way I can by describing what I see the path of love to be. When I look at this path, love really seems quite simple. Follow me through it, won't you?

The Path of Love

Have you ever seen a newborn baby in a mother's arms, a puppy, or a new kitten, who didn't have a

Chapter 4: The Path of Love (Cherish)

heart so wide open to the world that it was completely ready to receive love and absorb it, suck-it-up, and take-it-in? I would hate to be proven wrong on that one, but I think that is why I always want a new-born puppy in my home. (I have raised puppies; I have never had children.) There is something in that newness that opens something inside each one of us. When you look at them, something in you remembers. And when you remember, you remember, "Oh... yes." You're an open channel. Oh, yes, the memory of purity, the memory of welcoming... the memory of love.

As we get older, and we have our first love, what happens in that first romantic love? Doesn't the heart go: "Oh, yes" again? And we fall-in. We fall into love with one who opened the heart. Remember that the heart of love is simply stroked by the external, only then to be opened to the deep internal vast reaches of God's love, which pours through and wants to emanate through us more all the time.

Another part of the way in which love works here on earth (even though I think we are all embraced in love, in a capsule of love all the time) is that life's experiences make us think love went away— although it can't. On the front page of

The Path of God

Centerpoint[27] this month, my article about love states that "even when it feels as if it is gone, it is hungering to burst through so it is never gone." You can't get away from it. In beginning the path of love, then, we are all born into a sense of awe and wonder and hunger and openness and charm and joy and rapture in relation to love, whether born in the ghetto, or Ethiopia or Afghanistan; it applies to Christa McAuliffe[28]—all of us—Hitler, the Pope, Napoleon, Stalin, Lenin—all of us.

Then, as a part of the natural process, I am reminded of a poem by Wordsworth where he states, "Gradually shades of the prison house close round about us."

I am inclined to believe that we have looked at that occurrence and said, "What a shame that life does that to us."

My belief however is that this closing down is even a part of the design, the plan—God's plan is

---

[27] A periodical publication of Unity of Walnut Creek (Ed.)

[28] Christie McAuliffe is the famous American hero, astronaut, and school teacher that perished, along with six other crew members in the Space Shuttle Challenger tragedy, just a few days before this sermon was delivered. (Ed.)

Chapter 4: The Path of Love (Cherish)

to close the prison gates around us; and the necessity of that is, until love is tested, it cannot be known and realized. Strength is not made through ease. A good relationship is not empowered without some test. A deep friendship is not born out of ease. A powerful marriage, after fifty years, has been tempered by every hellish moment lived through—through which they were able to remain bonded.

So, the "shades of the prison house do close around us." And what are they? Where do they come from? It is the first time you went to suck from your mother's breast and some part of her life was demanding some other part of her—and she refused you and there was a closure. It was the first time you ran out into the street, and you didn't know what kind of a mess you were about to get in to, but the mother with the broader vision came out and grabbed you from in front of that car and said, "Get back inside you rotten kid! What are you doing?"

And you read that as rejection. It is the first time your little playmate didn't show up for the dance of playing in the mud—you felt rejected. And the shades of the prison house closed round about you. It is the first time you went to school and some teacher, instead of praising you, put you down. Little did you know—you deserved it.

And then I remember Anthony Seminara, my first love, in the third grade. In my opinion, Anthony was fickle. Rejection? Remember the first 'F' on your report card? And then it is falling in love with that first 'symphonic rose' and thinking that life is going to be fine now, I can get away from mom and dad... only to find that problems come up and things don't work out, that the football team or the 'A' on a report card is too important to him, and shades of the prison house close around.

And then maybe some of you reading this went further with it and you got married. And when you got married it was wonderful—five years of wonderful. And then the passion faded—the petal fell off the rose and the bloom went out, and you read it as rejection—no love. And gradually shades of the prison house are deepening. And then the first child that you probably didn't want or that you did want came along, and now the rejections are intensifying. You know it is hard to live lifelong. Isn't there a statement at Rossmoor[29]

---

[29] Rossmoor is a retirement community in Walnut Creek, CA. (Ed.)

Chapter 4: The Path of Love (Cherish)

that says, "Age takes courage; age takes strength." So, your children disappoint you. Maybe you lost a parent at a young age. Maybe you are the Smith family this morning and Mr. Smith isn't there anymore and it makes no sense—only rejection.

Now what happens in the human condition is that all of these experiences become a hardened form around us. Can't you feel it in parts of you? It comes out in funny ways too. How does it form? My brother and I almost did it at the airport last Thursday. We almost just coolly said, "Well, kid, see ya." And then the next time you see them, you don't dare poke your finger into the bubble of feeling again. And the next time you go to a movie, you look at it and say, "I'm not going to be touched by that." I think it happens a lot in adolescence. You go to church and someone says, "Reach out and hold the hand next to you."

And you say, "I won't touch their hand—that's my father—that's my mother—I don't touch."

Sometimes we show our avoidance of real deep feeling by being comical. You know... a quick, cute phrase. I was really badly damaged in 1978—badly damaged. In October, I can remember calling my brother and crying over the phone with

The Path of God

him in pain and saying to him, "God, Dick, it hurts."

He said, "Carol, just be glad you still have feelings."

The day I don't ever want to feel in me is the day I got bitter. But shades of the prison house do close around.

God has an amazing 'trip' going on here. We are all walking this path and it is the path of love: there are the friends; there are the fallen heroes; there are the fallen warriors; there are the people who didn't work out; there are the disappointments; there are the pains; there are the deaths; there are the miseries; there are the mistakes, the accidents, and the unable-to-be-explained parts of life. But what is amazing about it all is even though it may all cloud over, every so often (and I love this part of God) there will be a flash—a flash will show through the foliage, and it will penetrate itself into your heart and you will remember, again. It may happen here in a church service. You may even resent it. You may walk in here to Unity Center and cry, and you don't even understand it. Well, I'll tell you why it happened—because some of you stepped into that light, and it shone through all that bitterness and through that

Chapter 4: The Path of Love (Cherish)

hard shell and knocked the prison doors apart to give you remembrance that you were born into love.

You see, it is a part of love's mystery to take it away from you so that you will hunger for it once you find it again to make a commitment, "I will never, not love again! I am going to make a commitment to love! I am not going to listen only to the self-esteem movement that says to stand up and punch back when you are hit! I am going to leave a little bit inside me to say—LOVE. That's what I am committed to." That is why I wept when I heard that Russia sent condolences when the space shuttle shattered. Naturally the next day they returned to politics saying 'Star Wars'[30] is no good. But love flashed its light through for one second.

When that shaft of light pokes its way through the foliage, sometimes, if you are really lucky, when it pokes its beam through, something really raw is opened up inside as you say, "I only want love." Then your life is different. Some of you talk about that moment as your beginning of the spiritual

---

[30] This is a reference to USA President Ronald Reagan's proposed missile defense system. (Ed.)

path. Some of you fell in love. Some of you couldn't continue the way you were going. Some of you hit the bottom as alcoholics. Some of you fell too hard in love, and you couldn't sustain it. And from that time on, the rest of your life becomes a listening. Something happens inside your system—it got all alive and tingly and you began to want to hear love; and you became a sponge that only wanted to drink it in and then you begin one, long learning. First you will try to find it outside again. You will try to find it through me. You will try to fall in love again. You will try to get 'turned on' again to something— some new program, some seminar, some 'medicine show'. And if you are in the right place, all of those will say. "Not this… not me… not this… not this. You, you, you fall in love with you." What do we mean when we say to fall in love with you? We mean, discover the God within, discover the light that shines, and discover the memory of love that was given birth in you. And then as you learn it, you will learn some simple Truths in practicing love.

Simple Truths in Practicing Love

Love Is Not Self-Protection

Chapter 4: The Path of Love (Cherish)

This is probably the toughest of all, especially living in an age of self-esteem development and empowering people. Love is not about self-protection. And if you dare to have a relationship that is all you will ever learn. You cannot protect yourself. Here it is described perfectly in *The Velveteen Rabbit*. It is one of those wonderful classic stories about a stuffed animal who is trying to discover how to become real. And when you become 'real', you become love. (And remember, I am not talking about a love where you totally demoralize yourself or leave yourself wide open, because such love must begin with knowing how to love yourself. That is what you must cherish first.) But the rabbit is trying to discover what is real.

> *"What is REAL?" asked the Rabbit one day, when they were lying side by side near the nursery fender, before Nana came to tidy the room. "Does it mean having things that buzz inside you and a stick-out handle?" "Real isn't how you are made," said the Skin Horse. "It's a thing that happens to you. When a child loves you for a long, long time, not just to play with, but REALLY loves you, then you become Real." "Does it hurt?" asked the Rabbit. "Sometimes," said the Skin Horse, for he was always truthful. "When you are Real, you don't mind being hurt." "Does it happen all at once, like being wound up," he asked, "or bit by bit?" "It doesn't happen all at once," said the Skin Horse. "You become. It takes a long time. That's*

> *why it doesn't often happen to people who break easily, or have sharp edges, or who have to be carefully kept. Generally, by the time you are Real, most of your hair has been loved off, and your eyes drop out and you get loose in the joints and very shabby. But these things don't matter at all, because once you are Real you can't be ugly, except to people who don't understand."* [31]

Don't we hate this in our marriages? Don't we hate keeping-on becoming vulnerable? Don't we hate it in our work—keeping-on becoming vulnerable? Don't we hate it in our churches? We all have such conditions and limits on how a relationship with anything is going to go. It has to always go nice and easy. "Real isn't how you are made, it is a thing that happens to you when somebody loves you for a long, long time." Not just to play with, but to experience the pain. Then you become real. God, don't we all want to be carefully kept in our loving? But love won't let you if you would become real. Love is not about self-protection. We may not know what it is, but we know it is not about self-protection.

Love Is Not About Judging Others According To One's Self

---

[31] Margery Williams, *The Velveteen Rabbit*, (Running Press, 1981) pp. 13-15

Chapter 4: The Path of Love (Cherish)

And love is not about judging others according to one's self. I won't say anything more about that, but it is not about judging others according to one's self. It is amazing how we all want to change each other. I'll leave that as it is.

Love Is About Breaking One's Heart

Love is about breaking one's heart. I remember the first time my heart was broken. It happened when I was thirty years old. I had fallen very deeply in love with a married man. And I'll tell you—everything was pulling us to each other—sexuality, hunger. I went to visit him in his home town, and it was going to be the 'great engagement'. He came down to see me at a motel, and I was sitting there in my flagrant blue bikini bathing suit.

He walked down and looked at me and said, "You know, I am willing to spend this time with you and I haven't seen my child this week."

Something went "click, click, click" in me. We went up to the room and I sat down on the bed and looked at him and said, "I'm so scared to say to you what I must now say because I'm afraid my heart will break." I said those words. I looked at him and I said, "We can't go any further, we have to say good-bye." And my heart broke and I got bigger.

Sometimes when people say things that they say to me I feel as if I can't hear it one more time. Do you ever feel that way? Something inside me, automatically now, because I have worked at it, goes POP and I open up one more time. The heart got broken again.

Love Is About Cherishing

And then finally, love is about cherishing. I can't believe that as much as I love my little dog, Cindy, how many days go by that I never pick her up and hug her. I am finding that the older she gets and the closer it comes to our parting—which is going to be tough for me—the more I want to cherish her. I would have loved to have her here this morning to show her off to you—to have held her in my arms for you to see me cherish her. I don't know if I have told each of you how much I cherish you. I would like to tell all of you that individually.

I am just being an example—that is all I am being. Oh, God... don't let one of your loved ones go up on a spacecraft and not have said goodbye; not

Chapter 4: The Path of Love (Cherish)

have told them you cherish them.[32] Don't do that to yourself. Remember in the movie, _Terms of Endearment_: in the closing scene with the boy who hates his mother, she says, "I am not going to let you do that; I am not going to let you close me out and then feel sorry for the rest of your life." Well, that's remembering to cherish and sharing it without losing another minute.

3: Bless the Beasts celebration

---

[32] This is another reference to Christa McAuliffe's passing. (Ed.)

The Path of God

5: THE PATH OF LOVE (THE SHADOW)

February 9, 1986

Introduction

The previous lesson, "The Path of Love (Cherish)" concerned loving, the richness of loving, and cherishing each other in as many moments as possible. As we approach Valentine's Day, in our desire to 'be loving', it is clear that there is a tendency to believe that loving is a path of ease and to hope it will always be a path of ease.

We all know as we grow together that we are here to be loved and we are here to love. I think that is a philosophical commitment—I hope it is your commitment. Run those words inside you—"I am here to be loved and I am here to love." Just drench yourself in that idea for a moment, and feel your realization of the truth of that, the factuality of that. "I am here to be loved and I am here to love." Obviously, it is an inspired statement, but the challenge is that it is very difficult to realize—to make real. The tendency in our relationships—whether with our church, our work, our children, our mates, our money, or our professions—is to not know how to bring forth that love. Over the years, we gain different impressions as to whether this idea is really the truth, that we are here to be loved, and if it is the truth we still experience that the love does get blocked, as mentioned in the last lesson: "shades of the prison house close around." So we get blocked from our compassionate love; we experience rejection; we experience other people's anger; we experience our own anger, etc. The tendency is to find it so frustrating and so few people in the world are willing to receive or give love totally, that we begin to judge that the loving part of our life is not available as hoped. And we question the validity of loving… are all parts of us lovable? Is love for all of the parts? What is it that blocks us, stops us from loving?

The Shadow

This area of loving is not the easiest one to talk about. It is usually called the shadow—a psychological concept; and the shadow exists within each one of us. To enter into it, consider your relationships and let them rise into your mind, including those parts of your relationships that you usually want to leave out, that you usually

Chapter 5: The Path of Love (The Shadow)

don't want to talk about; those parts that make you vulnerable, fearful, or make you crazy.

Your words will say, "God, this part of this person drives me crazy," or, "it is going to drive me to drink, I can't stand this in this other person."

Let them all run through your mind. Where are those places in your relationship where you find yourself annoyed—continually annoyed? You go into work every day and that personality continues to create anger inside you. Of course, we think they caused it, but the truth is that the anger is ours—it is our gift to ourselves, but the tendency is to suppress it, to ignore it; to believe it isn't right to feel like that or to express it, or the timing isn't right. All those may be true, but just for a moment let's take a look at those situations, those personalities with whom we feel that annoyance.

Isn't it a classic scenario about all of us that we may go to many different relationships, many different jobs, many different neighborhoods, and many different countries, yet no matter where we go, it remains the same? We pick-up our baggage, we change our houses, we change the personalities, we walk in, put down our baggage, and after a few months, there they appear all over again. It is like a movie theater and the same movie show keeps coming around in front of us, we sit there eating our popcorn and the same issue continues to come up causing fury, anger, self-disgust, or guilt at feeling that way. Then we go to a church service and we hear people saying, "Let's love, let's cherish" and we go home to do the cherishing and the loving—and the same person and issue, etc. rises inside and the fuse blows—the bomb goes off. Love, as we believe it is, is lost! Then, of course, we all carry this into our external world and begin to understand why fuses and bombs are created: the external world is no more than a bigger screen for all of us to play out the smaller, inner experiences of our life. So the Russians end up hating the United States, the Communists hate the Capitalists, the Nazis hate the Jews and the truth is that we are all working through our hunger to be loved, our feeling that we want to love, but we don't know how. The issue behind it all is that we will not encounter the dark side, the shadow within; we would rather repress it, ignore it, and project it on to everybody else out there rather than look at it within ourselves. Some of us have children that drive us crazy, bosses who drive us crazy, or situations that drive us crazy. And some of this happens, of course, in just the opposite way.

Chapter 5: The Path of Love (The Shadow)

Sometimes it isn't people driving us crazy, but we may find that we keep becoming attached and falling in love with the same personality type. What is occurring in this instance is that we are all hungering for that part of ourselves, but in this case we are projecting it out as love of someone else. This time the love is not a detached kind of loving or an easy kind of loving, rather it becomes a painful kind of loving where we can never get what we want. And we find ourselves beating on that other in order to try to get from them what we want. But, once again, it is that unclaimed part of ourselves that we can't claim and honor within ourselves. In my job people use me, as they often use their leaders, to project their incomplete selves upon. Then they beat those leaders down to become what they want them to become without recognizing what they are really saying is, "I want to become that within myself."

A Personal Example

This story from life is remarkable, and only as I prepared this lesson, did I take a look at this part of my life in this way. All through my life (and this is just an example) I had had difficulty with quiet people. I am not a quiet person. I am primarily extroverted—'quietness' I do alone. But, I had bumped into people who 'scared' me because of their quietness. Do you know what that is like? If asked a question, there would be nothing coming forward, there was no response and the way they handled life was with this deep quiet. I tried to understand that 'silence is golden' and it didn't feel golden at all for me. Yet there was this tremendous attraction to them, I wanted to be around them, and I wanted to understand them. And then I would get near them and there would be something inside me that would feel blocked, inadequate, and incomplete. I didn't know how to make contact. I can remember a portion of my life at home where sometimes we would invite guests.

I remember often my mother and father saying after the dinner, "God, they don't say anything, do they, has the cat got their tongue? They don't have any substance."

So I would work both ways with them, I would be deeply attracted, and I wouldn't know what to do. The only thing I knew was to 'pound in', go for them—find them. And, of course, I am their shadow because their fear was my opposite nature trying to find them. They desired to be left alone and let them be just as they are.

In 1976, as a part of one of the most dramatic spiritual journeys of my life, I was dragged into

Chapter 5: The Path of Love (The Shadow)

my silent self, and it was full of terror. I did everything in my power to try to get away from that, to try to get back to the good old personable Carol, the 'personality kid', and yet it kept taking me deeper and deeper and deeper. I ended up in a Dark Night of the Soul[33] period, the mystical dark night of the soul, and I hung out in quietness for three years and regained my sense of completion with it and comfort with it within myself so that it no longer frightened me. It took me nearly all of six years to come to terms with it.

The Shadow Theory

Here is a reading from a book entitled, *The Feminine in Jungian Psychology and in Christian Theology*:

> *The shadow is the image used by Jung to describe those contents in ourselves that we repress because they are unacceptable, such as tawdry thoughts, unbounded power aspirations, secret faults.*
>
> *[Do you know about "secret faults, tawdry thoughts," the faults and the secrets you won't share with anybody that*

---

[33] A reference to the poem, *La noche oscura del alma,* Saint John of the Cross, where he described the deep hardships a Soul endures to reach God. (Ed.)

keep you from intimacy? "They certainly wouldn't love me if I... " "I certainly wouldn't love me if I... ."C.R.K.]

On the collective level, the shadow is often personified as the devil; on the individual level it is always represented by someone of the same sex whom we dislike and find irritating or even hateful.

[Why do you think we have so much success in our traditional churches that are using the devil to project their own uncomfortable feelings upon, to build a whole movement that then is projected upon all those 'bad guys' out there? As a result they refuse to take on their own shadow. The way of our society has been to escape the shadow, to ignore it, to repress it. This lesson is entitled, "The Path of the Shadow" and the secret is to take on your shadow, rather than projecting it, standing aloof from it. C.R.K.]

Our first contact with our own shadow is usually through projecting it onto others; we see qualities we do not recognize in ourselves as belonging only to them. This projection can happen with positive or negative qualities, but usually what we reject in others is what we do not accept in ourselves. Racial conflict is a broader manifestation of this, as are the mutual projections of Communists and Capitalists.[34]

---

[34] Ann Belford Ulanov, <u>The Feminine in Jungian Psychology and in Christian Theology</u>, (Northwestern University Press, 1971) p. 33-34

Chapter 5: The Path of Love (The Shadow)

4: We live in Shadow and in Light

I would like to give you some examples. Yesterday we had a dramatic experience near the end of our Lay Ministry training in which I shared with people the process of reaching into others, doing prayer counseling, listening, and allowing people to express themselves. The person who shared the experience shared some powerful inner fears and parts of herself that were very frightening to her. It came through her as tears and a lot of revelation; it was remarkable how everybody was affected with the courage of this woman who shared her shadow. She was able to share her shadow because she was sitting with somebody who fully accepted that shadow and did not want to alter it, change it, pray it into something, manipulate it or control it for the 'good of the world'. I watched, however, a person who was taking the class as an observer, become so uncomfortable with the shadow, no doubt used to praying 'something' out of existence, sat with eyes closed for the rest of the meeting. I am sure this person was focused inside trying to pray that shadow out of existence.

Think about yourself, is that what you do? Is that what you want to do? Is that your tendency? When you see your dark side come up, when you see it in yourself, do you try to get rid of it? I had a young man come to see me this week who shared his experience of an LSD trip. I happen to be one of those ministers in society who believes that drugs can be one of the most significant and powerful first steps into potential spirituality and re-awakening the spiritual life that people can use. I do not support ongoing drug use; I do appreciate those who have used it and its effect in awakening parts of consciousness that have caused them to want to pursue spirituality in

Chapter 5: The Path of Love (The Shadow)

deeper ways. This person shared with me that while on an LSD trip he had encountered his dark side. As he encountered his dark side, which came forth as a 'black witch', (it can also come up in dreams too, it doesn't have to come out as external personalities), his whole compulsion was to run as fast as he could and get away from it. And he had come to me to say, "Would you help me re-meet the black witch?" Our tendency, however, is to run away. Look at yourself; listen to yourself; notice yourself; watch yourself. How are you using this part of you to separate yourself from humanity, to keep yourself safe and looking good? Then we wonder why we lose relationships, why they blow up, why they don't continue, why we come to believe that we can't have an ongoing relationship. And the truth is we won't let ourselves be known, not to ourselves, and not to others. And if you are working on the spiritual path, as I believe I am committed—right or wrong—then what we are wanting is relationships who will let us be all that we are, because we are studying becoming all that we are.

I have had to address the experience in the past two or three months where I have, much to my amazement as a minister, discovered that some people don't want all of me. I won't give you the specifics, but in two instances, I walked into situations where I shared my shadow and you know what was reflected back?

"You're a minister, don't share your shadow. No, we want our minister to be pure and saint-like, removed from all that."

But that is not the ministry to which I am committed. I won't play out that game with society—hiding my shadow. I have angry parts; I have fearful parts; and I am going to express the strength and the courage to say, "Here I am—all of me—and I know God loves me and that is why I have the courage to let you see it all."

Earlier this week I learned that a church in Santa Rosa, whose minister I met, had set out on a building program this past year. Because the church leaders held the vision, but denied their fear of not being able to raise the money, they failed. They went $25,000 in the hole and the minister had to stop doing full time [ministry] work and is now working part time. They buried their shadow. Is that what your relationship is built upon? Are you afraid to share your whole self? Are you afraid to take it out from underneath the covers and allow yourself to be seen? And are you building relationships built upon chicken awareness—I'll play chicken and you play chicken

Chapter 5: The Path of Love (The Shadow)

and maybe we can hold each other, in the fear you might see who I am and then we won't want each other! And then we suffocate and we die, nothing moves, and it all becomes still, unexposed, and fermenting garbage.

In another example, I would like to share with you how we will run to that which does not expose our shadow and try to remain with it because it is so easy. My brother visited me during the month of January. My brother is my 'Siamese twin'. He is four years younger, but he is my Siamese twin. And when I walked into the house to see him, (it was the first time I spent a long time with him in probably twenty-five years) we ran in to each other's arms. It was like, "Oh yes," it felt easy. And as he spent four weeks with me, there was never any disorder in the relationship. The 'Siamese twins' met, and they bonded again. And I adore him, and I love him; and do you know why? Because he is easy and he is just like me! We 'hang around' and listen to music together, we don't have to talk, we can go skiing together, we can build together, and as we work and share our pain and our stories and our whole internal process, we feel our totality. There is quietness, and sound, and a marvelous intertwining of relationship. When he left, I missed him as if somebody had cut off my arm.

But I realized that through Richard Knox, I will not grow—it is too easy. But do I ever want to re-create him!

Another Truth: The Shadow Also Provides Protection

There is a wonderful song that sings, "Turn around, turn around." It exemplifies the possibility, the other truth of the shadow. I've shared with you the dark side, the difficult side of it: the passions, the angers, the frustrations, the resentments, the hatred, and the loving passions, but there is another truth about shadows and that is in the heat of the day, the shadows protect. I happened to watch *The Love Boat* on TV last night because it was filmed in Egypt. Jean Stapleton kept saying a phrase in Egyptian and it really fits Egypt; the phrase is, "Where is the shade?" If we turn around and walk in to the shadow, the shadow ultimately provides protection—and you must have the courage to recognize this part of the shadow if you would walk its path in spirituality. If you walk into your shadow, it provides protection, and clarity, like the old radio program, "The Shadow Knows." Emerson[35]

---

[35] Ralph Waldo Emerson (Ed.)

Chapter 5: The Path of Love (The Shadow)

states, "We have to keep our bloated nothingness out of the divine circuits." Since we have believed that the shadow is so powerful, so ominous we have hung on to it rather than letting it go, and thereby filled the Divine circuits. And letting it go, only happens as you walk into it. Turn around... walk into the shadow!

The Bible poets seemed to recognize this. I would like to read to you from Psalm 17:

> *Keep me as the apple of the eye; hide me in the shadow of thy wings. From the wicked [parts of myself] who would despoil me, my deadly enemies who surround me. (Psalm 17:8)*

The feeling of this Psalm is that God provides the shadow in which to be protected.

> *He who dwells in the shelter of the Most High, who abides in the shadow of the Almighty. (Psalm 91:1)*

> *"These are only a shadow of what is to come, but the substance belongs to the Christ." (Colossians 1:17)*

'In the shadow' is the substance of the Christ!

And now, to return to <u>*The Feminine in Jungian Psychology and in Christian Theology*</u>, because it may put this recognition into contemporary language:

> *Without a shadow we are flat, two-dimensional. The shadow's darkness grounds us, adding depth, perspective, and three dimensions. We take on substance and have a history. If conscious ego adaptation is around negative and inferior qualities, the shadow will then present us with neglected positive potentialities. It is not the shadow's own nature that occasions its menacing appearance, but rather our treatment of it. As we begin to give some attention and care to channeling these neglected aspects of ourselves, they become less threatening and more helpful to us.*[36]

The key to the shadow is to turn around, walk into it. Remember that it has a role, that it is some part of us that we learned long ago not to love within ourselves and the only way to love it is to enter in.

We can get other images from our contemporary society. Maybe it is becoming more comfortable with the shadow in its 100 year recent history as a part of us. There was a song performed by Simon and Garfunkle in the 60's: one line says, "Hello darkness, my old friend." I'm begging you all this morning to walk into your shadow. I don't have anything more to offer—you have to walk into it. You must walk in through your relationships; you

---

[36] Ulanov, *The Feminine in Jungian Psychology and in Christian Theology*, p. 35

Chapter 5: The Path of Love (The Shadow)

must dare to share all of you, and as you do, you will build a relationship that will allow you the freedom to be all that you are. This summer, when I took my trash to the dump in Winthrop, I fell in love with the T-shirt label the man wore: "Garbage is beautiful". There is a whole new rage in our country, at least in the San Francisco area; it is no longer the Cabbage Patch Kids, but the "Garbage Pail Kids". It seems as if our society is beginning to say, "C'mon, let's come out of our shadow, let's come out of our darkness, and let's honor our greasy selves, our dark selves, and share it!" And the recognition, only about one hundred years old in psychological history, is that not until we handle that part of ourselves and make it overt and exposed can we continue the human race in its evolutionary process.

The Shadow is Painful

In closing, I would like to share this with you the reason we don't want to enter into our shadow is because our dark side is painful. Nobody wants the pain; and here are two personal experiences from my life in the past week to exemplify this. A few days ago, I was on my way out, rushing to come here for some activity. At that moment a window for the attic arrived, brought by a delivery man. The window cost $93.[10]. All I had was a hundred dollar bill. I stood out there on the grass and realized that I didn't have the change and that the driver didn't have the change. Our lives were being pulled in every direction. I looked at my roommate and said, "Can you go get the change?"

She looked at me and said, "I'm too busy, I can't."

And I said, "You've got to go and get the change!" which is my projection of my belief that I am more important than she is in that situation. The anger comes up when she doesn't acknowledge that. At that instant we entered into the typical power play, and yet, all that is going on is my shadow at work. Now to the pain: I walked into the house and lay on my bed, looked at myself and saw me for what I am; and I felt mortified, that is the word, mortified. That was the pain—recognizing my shadow and who I am. When she returned in a few moments, she tried to explain—for no doubt she had her experience in seeing her part—and I couldn't stand having her look at me because that part of me was so uncomfortable. But I had made a move. I let the shadow in, and I saw it, and I experienced the pain, and it moved me forward.

I have another very special relationship in my life. This week I realized that it was having real

Chapter 5: The Path of Love (The Shadow)

struggles. The struggles were based upon the fact that I am very angry about certain parts of the relationship. One day this week, I decided to share my anger. I had never expressed it to this degree before. I shared it and I shared it; it must have been a three hour marathon. And the other person shared theirs and shared theirs and shared theirs. I went home and woke the next morning, and as I lay there in bed, I felt totally hopeless, because I could not see how the relationship could continue. I then reached deeper and deeper in to my pain and in to my shadow and I recognized that I must give up my demands. (And as you read this, remember that was only my learning—don't take this as a teaching to give up your demands—it is my learning only. Maybe your learning is to become more demanding.) Then I watched in my mind's eye the whole form of the relationship crumble... crumble... and the horror in me was that I could not possibly live with it the way it is, and I felt that I would be in for a long period of pain. Then something said, "But the pain is the only way through." And I became willing. Within three hours, I was abundant internally.

To close let me share a major experience I had with my shadow about eight years ago. I met my shadow head-on. I think once you meet your shadow head-on, then you still have to come to grips with its minute-by-minute expression in this relationship—this situation. But you never run from it again. In this instance, I was overwhelmed by fear for over a year, and it led to tremendous anxiety. One day I went to a counselor and the counselor said, "Let's go into the fear." I was scared to death. If you think fear is bad, you should be afraid of fear.[37] So we went 'inside', and the counselor said, "What is the fear?"

The fear became a spider immediately. I didn't want to touch it. (When I was a little girl, five years old, there was a spider in the basement and my mother tried to get me to not fear the spider. I couldn't go near it to even kill it then.) So the spider came in and an amazing thing happened; it invited me to go into its house and have tea. Crazy, right? Well, we went into its house, a darling tree house, and it had lovely arm chairs that were very comfortable. We sat there and talked and had tea in porcelain china cups. We shared, and I don't remember what we shared, but

---

[37] Carol Ruth is encouraging us to think non-dualistically and simply accept fear as a natural reaction to the unknown. From that perspective, we are free to enter into fear and dispel it. If you do not have this perspective, it is natural and okay to be afraid. (Ed.)

Chapter 5: The Path of Love (The Shadow)

I know that because I stayed there with the spider—something marvelous happened—I became comfortable. And, when the conversation was all over (the intellect has nothing to do with this), we came out from the spider's house into the yard. I stooped down and picked up the spider and I wanted to put the spider in my pocket because I had fallen in love with it—with my fear.

And the spider said to me, "No you can't keep me, I have to go teach others elsewhere." And I wept.

The Path of God

6: THE PATH OF NON-DUALITY

February 23, 1986

The Dualistic Way—A Possibility

This is probably the most difficult lesson I have given in the fifteen years that I have been in the ministry. To invite you into the considerations of this material, I am sure you recognize that living in a dualistic world is a deadly sport and game. The difficulty is that while living in a dualistic world, life and its rituals and its personalities end up being right or wrong — good or bad; for instance, if a person is unkind then we don't recognize that in the same instant they can also be showing love. In our relationships, our minds cast us into the thought that if someone is right, then their opposite must be wrong; if someone is unkind, then they cannot also be showing love; if they are abrupt, then certainly they cannot also be gentle.

The Path of God

We live out the model of white versus black, the good guys against the bad, and the Force against Darth Vader[38]. Our lives live on a stage where we act out the dark side and the light side, with the belief the black is wrong and the light is the desirable. Then we live our lives trying to jump from one side to the other, tending to think that our spirituality has something to do with the white side—the light side—and that our negativity or 'devil' has to do with the dark side. Consequently, we are forever living out the battle of polarities, continually jumping from one opposite back to the other. Our verbal and thinking processes perpetuate this in word choices such as "better than", "worse than", "more than", and "less than", creating deeper polarity or forcing us into having to make decisions. We talk about having to make choices, controlling outcomes, and live certain kinds of realities, etc.

The process forces us to act out annihilation and exorcism. Why? Because if you live and only want to be in the 'white side', then the [dualistic] choice is to annihilate the dark side, to exorcise the dark

---

[38] The Force and Darth Vader are references to the _Star Wars Trilogy_, a movie series by George Lucas that shows the forces of good and evil clashing in a futuristic universe. (Ed.)

Chapter 6: The Path of Non-Duality

side, and to make one's decisions based on always wanting to be on the white side. The process continues in excruciating fashion as we see the opposing side as a threat, something to be fought and defended against. Consequently through our words and actions, we fight with relationships, organizations, principles, and through causes as we find a way to play out the light side against the dark, the good against the bad, and the right against the wrong. It becomes intensely painful because we feel compelled to get rid of one in order for the other to survive. As you can see, war then becomes the world activity to express the antagonism experienced in trying to let the good, the white, and the right win.

At times, and especially if you understand non-duality, you can stand way back from these inner and outer wars in the elevated position looking at both with a 'click' in your tongue as you recognize its absurdity! You can even be in the midst of a fight, wailing for your rights as a human being, and in an instant experience a reality that sees the absurdity. Then you may find yourself even laughing at you! (Even though you knew you were right!).

Let me take a look now at some of the ways in which we act-out 'duality'. We may set out to discover our 'self'. My sense is, in that search, we are trying to discover this wonderful self so that we can hold on to it, define it, so that finally we might come to know who we are. As if the self is something one can hold onto, define, and put into concrete. Our way to this self is often a series of confrontations wherein we determine "I am not this, not that, and so this doesn't belong to me and that doesn't belong to me, nor this etc." A battle is fought with those parts that do not belong, the tendency is, however, the more you seek to free yourself of those parts, the more you attract them into your life through personalities, fears, and discomforts. The struggle is incredible; it often leaves you thinking you know who you are, but through the destruction and elimination of all your opposition and excitement! Nondualistically, however, the truth is that the self cannot be defined, confirmed, confined, or put into solidarity under any conditions. Because the self is a constantly molding, shaping, and consistently changing, that 'something' will never allow itself to be grasped or held onto. We must instead give it up, rather than preserve it.

Another way we live this, these dualistic processes, show in our treatment of illnesses. If we become ill, we believe that 'better' is to get healthier. To enhance this, we build religions

Chapter 6: The Path of Non-Duality

which help us get better, get healthier. As you read this, be careful because you may find your mind beating back at me and that will happen through dualistic thinking. That appears in a question such as, "Well, isn't 'healthy' all right?" The question says that you assume I am in polarity and the minute I open my mouth I am thinking in duality. Of course we do this to each other because we built our thinking processes on duality. So nobody can escape. What is forgotten in duality thinking is that it is possible that I could say two things, one verbalized and the other necessarily heard within, and I can mean both of them with equal power. In this example, I could be saying that it is possible we could become ill and believe we could get better, and we could also believe we could become worse, and there would be no preference about the end result. As you hear this idea coming into you, if you feel a little frightened and that some portion of your structure is being taken from you, it is a justified fear. I am taking away your structure, your solidarity—something for you to put your feet into; something to hold on to; something to make you feel 'good' about who you are and standing 'fixed' in that position. However, if you remain in such a fixed position, it could be more difficult and dangerous over the long run than willingly becoming fluid, moving, and creative.

Another way in which we live this out in our daily lives is through our children's difficulties. For instance, in school, we tend to compare our children with all the 'A' students. How many of us have grasped the possible thought that maybe children grow and move through certain parts of their lives at different rates and on different schedules? For instance, I lived-out my adolescence in my mid-thirties; I never touched it at twelve. But regardless, I had to still live-out adolescence. When our children don't meet the world's schedule, and we consider them wrong (rather than right for themselves), we are immersed in duality.

The jig of polarity goes on and on. To be or not to be: caught in the middle of a decision our words are, "Should I or shouldn't I? Do I go or don't I go? Do I stay or don't I stay? Do I love or don't I love? Am I loving? Is this love? Was that love?" We also live between life and death, one better than the other, you know. There is the polarity: to build the bomb or ban the bomb. Such a wonderful one! We end up antagonizing the ones who are building it and honor the ones who are banning it. Another in our present culture is the right to life and the right to choice. That's a thumbnail of how duality goes. So, let's leave it there and take a look at another way of being with life.

Non-Duality—Also Possible

Your eye is the lamp of your body; when your eye is sound, your whole body is full of light; but when it is not sound, your body is full of darkness. Therefore, be careful lest the light in you be darkness. If then your whole body is full of light, having no part dark, it will be wholly bright, as when a lamp with its rays gives you light.[39]

"If your eye is the lamp of your body, when your eye is sound, your whole body is full of light." First, let's look at how we have interpreted these words—usually dualistically. Our desire has been to be what Jesus suggests: "If I could only get my eye sound… if I could only get it 'full of light'." The way we have attempted to do this has been to get on the light side; we hoped to accomplish this by thinking good thoughts, being kind or good, treating our kids right, or going for the 'gold' etc. Our thought has been that anytime we moved into the dark side, then we were out of the light, and we were missing the mark of being perfect as Jesus would have us. However, I do not think that

---

[39] Luke 11:34-35

is what these words are saying. I think there is a possibility that something else is being said. What if 'soundness' of the eye is only to see what is? What if the light that Jesus is talking about, what if the eye that is sound or single, is the eye that stands transcendent, watching, and seeing both the light and dark? Light is the opposite of dark and there is another aspect within, one we could call bright—one that sees light/dark, good/bad. And that brightness is the single eye. The single eye is not to get into the light and get rid of the darkness, but rather to be the bright that sees both light and dark without preference. The eye only has to see what is to be single.

Now, watch how that concept works in you, for once again it may take away your structure, your support system, or your solidarity based upon believing you could know you were 'right'. If you do feel the ground moving out from underneath you based upon your having nothing to stand on, my hope is that by the end of this lesson, you will have been given something to stand on and that something will be movement.

There is a final consideration in this interpretation of Luke. What if the only darkness is the assumption that there could be darkness; which even of itself cannot be darkness, because there is

Chapter 6: The Path of Non-Duality

no place where you can be separate in God's Universe—even in thinking darkness is not a part of God's Universe and design. To say it another way: what if the only darkness is the assumption that you are in darkness, which is the subtle belief that you think you know what is right or wrong—and even that is a part of the design of the (your) process, because it is a part of the whole for you/anyone to have that question. This means that you/anyone cannot ever be not in God.

Reference from Physics

These paragraphs will present material from new physics. They will, in most instances, not be direct quotes, but a general interpretation from my understanding. At the same time, I would suggest you read *The Spectrum of Consciousness* by Ken Wilber. I spent the summer with this book and I kept getting up from my chair by the side of the river, walking with it, because it was 'blowing' me out of who I was into more of who I was becoming.

The Heisenberg theory came along in the early part of this [20th (Ed.)] century. It is a conceptual/attitudinal changing from Newtonian thinking, which had convinced humanity that there was a way to say that something outside of us was more real than something inside of us. Further, we could set up a belief system (and a correspondent legal system, a psychological system, and even a right/wrong spiritual system) that could prove the 'out there' was right or wrong because it had a separate reality from the one who perceived. The foundational thinking, based upon Newton's system of physics, began to come to a screeching halt in the early 1900s. We, in our spiritual awareness now in the 1980s, must catch up with this shift in information since a lot of our thinking is based upon processes which no longer apply; yet that thinking continues in us human beings and we continue to build our lives based upon it. Furthermore, there are millions of people also building their lives upon this old thinking, and you and I bump up against them all the time.

Let's take a look at this new thinking. The new thinking simply says that it is impossible to determine what is outside, for indeed, there is no reality outside of us; there is only the reality that is inside us and that reality sees all as it is, knows all as it is, and perceives all as it is. The seer, knower, perceiver is the internal consciousness of the one who sees. Now, be careful, many of us have taken this belief system and stated, "Straighten out the consciousness and then you will get reality

Chapter 6: The Path of Non-Duality

straight." But that still separates. There is nothing to get straight: the internal consciousness sees reality which is right and wrong/good and bad, in its own way. The consciousness merely sees, beholds. There is nothing to argue about or prove for whoever sees is right in his/her own way and so is everyone else. Heisenberg came to the realization that the minute an object is determined as a separate reality outside of us—it is being formed by the consciousness looking at it. That object in turn is changing, as it is looked at and as it is seen, since nothing is static. It is like bobbing for an apple that you have already defined; you cannot. Feel that? It changes too quickly, it is moving too quickly—you cannot hold on to anything—all is moving. I am changing this instant. You cannot count on me. You cannot count on my mind. 'Who I am' is you—not me. There is no separation. I am not right or wrong, nor are you. We are what we are—different, changing, fluid, and becoming, etc.

A person described sitting in their room one day and looking down the hall at a picture on the wall. As they looked at it, the sun was coming in through a window casting onto the picture a reflection of a part of the hall and a fern. Their statement was, "So I didn't see the real picture." What is communicated here is an attempt to say there is something real out there, and when I get my 'thinking straight' then reality will be straight. What is being stated is that the real picture is the one on the wall which will be seen when the seer or the picture is purified and refined without a reflection upon it. There is another truth—the picture with the reflection on it is the real picture. That is non-duality thinking. Feel that? It is what it is.

Get it in your lives! IT IS WHAT IT IS—there is NO right or wrong out there—there is no out there—it is in YOU! And there is nothing to be 'cleaned-up' inside you either—because you cannot see 'wrong', because God does not see wrong and the one who is seeing through you IS God—the seer is God. I am excited about this, I am intense about this. This could be life-changing if you grasp this inner way because it will free you to simplicity, to seeing life simply as it is without control or manipulation, etc.

Consider a triangle that could also be seen as a pyramid with a base. Most of us live our lives caught at the base, between good/bad, and right/wrong, trying to figure it out, arguing it

Chapter 6: The Path of Non-Duality

through: who's on first, and what's on second?[40] When one moves to ascendant thinking, non-duality thinking, you realize it is not possibility thinking. Possibility thinking plays with the values at the base, whereas ascendant thinking creatively, significantly, and dynamically helps move one towards non-duality. It sits at the point of 'Bright' and does not deny the base activities—it plays in them. It relishes in and enjoys them; it is charmed by them; entertained by them. But, it sits at the apex and it sees it for what it is. And be careful; it even sees its judgment for what it is. It doesn't try to get rid of judgment. It doesn't try to get rid of good or bad, right or wrong—it just sees it for what it is.

One final consideration in capturing this vision of non-duality, it seems as if we have assumed that we were the object and that the one who sees the object is ourselves. For example, as you read this material, you know you are an object because you can see yourself from inside reading this material. There is an object and an 'I' watching you, the

---

[40] This is a reference to Abbot's and Costello's, comedic skit "Who's on First?", Reverend Knox is implying that working and arguing at the base of dualistic living is just as comedic, circular and ridiculous, but also as entertaining as the famous skit. (Ed.)

object. However, something has been left out of our thinking and our awareness in even this. It is, in order for you to behold an 'I' that is watching you read a book, there also has to be an 'I' that is watching the 'I' that reads the book. And the deepest mystical question that can be asked is, "Who is the 'I' that watches the 'I' reading the book?" The 'I' that is watching the 'I' that is reading the book is the apex that is not out of this ballgame, but fully incorporated in this ballgame, creating the ballgame, designing every part of the puzzle in the ballgame, intimately involved in the whole ballgame, caring for the whole ballgame. Feel it! Live it! It is exciting.

> *You cannot look at what 'Is', for it cannot become an object to the mind, nor for that matter, can it be a subject. What 'Is' that which can never be a subject or an object? Thus, the moment you look with your relative (subject-object-oriented) mind, what 'Is' is gone because you have tried to make it an object, and that won't work. The relative mind cannot apprehend this reality; only a non-relative mind sees because what 'Is' is equally non-reflective or non-self-conscious.*[41]

---

[41] Bernadette Roberts, *The Experience of No-Self*, (Iroquois House, 1982) p. 68

Chapter 6: The Path of Non-Duality

I hope you can feel that. It is showing that living and having no sense of oneself is not an object watching itself; it has become the watcher and the object is gone. When you live with this non-dualistic knowing, you do not have a sense of yourself. It is analogous to a performer who has done their work so well, studied the tools of the trade so well, built those responses so intimately into their system—they have learned how to make love; they have learned how to love; they have learned how to bear children; they have raised children; they have done their work; they have fought their battles and they are still fighting their battles. Then at some special moments in life, moments of great wonder which increase as one "gets living down pat, into simplicity," one gets so free of the self that one becomes only the Watcher and then there is no self and one just is. That is the essence of living. That is the dance. Come with me—feel it. If you can feel it, capture a glimpse of it—you do not really have to do too much except continual meditation and ongoing prayer in order to develop it until it becomes an attitude of living.

Synthesis

You see, if you enter into the non-dualistic world, then you enter into a world where there is both good and bad, right and wrong AND there is something as well that wraps it. If you live this concept, you do not live in an either or world, you live in an 'as well' world as well.

When you live in a non-dualistic world, you still live in the dualistic world, and you live in a world where 'but' is not so important, thus 'and' becomes important. When you live in this non-dualistic world, you will be able to see that it is possible for a person to be loving AND angry. Oh, God, if we could have been raised as children to know that love and anger can fit side by side in the same moment as it is given to us. And when you live in this non-dualistic world, every moment comes into one instant and all 'nows' are here—the past is now here—the future is now here—it is all here in this one moment—my life and death are here, and my reincarnation—all here, now.

Action in Duality?

Many people, when hearing this concept say, "Well, what will I do for the rest of my life if I just live in the now?! I have spent my whole life trying to get over on the white side and get rid of those bad guys. What will get me out of bed in the morning—there will be nothing to go for, no challenges—you took them away, Knox." Well, give me a few more minutes and I might give you a glimpse.

Inspiration

Yesterday morning, I was out running. I live in Antioch; and Antioch is a 'mixed message' kind of town—a great place for non-dualists. It is not 'upper class suburbia', but a mixed combination of everything and everyone. As one runs through the streets of Antioch, you see fleabag houses and exquisite old Victorians, bars, and old falling down places. Then, every so often you run by and see something that someone poured their heart into and gave their life to in order to express some inner moment of beauty. In so doing, I don't think they were 'out' for anything. I don't think they were going for any great goal or purpose. I don't think they were 'for' anything... probably they were saying, "Let me express myself here." And as I ran by, I was inspired by the glimpse of beauty in this mixed message of Antioch. You could be an inspiration just for who you are, not because you set out to inspire, but just because you lived your life as it is/was!

There is a man who runs down my street in front of my house every day—he is "nuttier than a fruitcake." He looks demented. He goes down to the neighborhood cafe where I occasionally eat breakfast and hangs out with the 'gurus' of Antioch. He wanders in, in his demented way, and when he comes in, my God—he brings in light. You see, if he does know he is demented, it does not matter—he is what he is, and he is an inspiration to everybody in that coffee shop. You could be an inspiration, just hang your life on being an inspiration not because you tried to be an inspiration, but just because you lived your life as it is/was! How about it? Who will know? Who will write about you fifty years from now? Nobody. Who will care? Nobody.

What's the Purpose, the Goal?

Another criticism of such a message has been, "Well, there is no purpose or goal." What would you do with your life, what would you seek for? What work would you get in? How much money would you make? Ram Dass says it in words like this:

When you come to this point of non-duality, and the question is asked, 'What is your purpose—what is your goal?' the simple answer is, that you do everything in the moment as if it had infinite meaning, knowing full well it

Chapter 6: The Path of Non-Duality

has absolutely none.[42]

They have told us that the last words said from planet Earth to the Challenger which crashed were: "Full throttle ahead." And the pilot said, "Roger." You're not out for the prize; it doesn't matter if you even get into orbit... but you just must MOVE. Now. In the instant.

A god can do it. But tell me, how can a man follow his narrow road through the strings? A man is split. And where two roads intersect inside us, no one has built the Singer's Temple. [The Singer's Temple is Non-Duality-- C.R. Knox]

Writing poetry as we learn from you is not desiring, not wanting something that can ever be achieved. To write poetry is to be alive. For a god that's easy. When, however, are we really alive? And when does he turn the earth and the stars so they face us? Yes, you are young, and you love, and the voice forces your mouth open—that is lovely, but... learn to forget that breaking into song. It doesn't last; Real singing is a different movement of air. Air moving around

---

[42] Ram Dass is a spiritual teacher, formerly Richard Alpert, who was a professional associate of Timothy Leary at Harvard University. He is famous for his foundational work, <u>Be Here Now.</u>

The Path of God

nothing. A breathing in a god. A wind.[43]

I hope you can get a feel for that poem. Purpose is hanging around to let the wind blow through you—not because you fell in love or because you had the 'exquisite minute', or because you got inspired, but because you were hanging around, and you got blown through because you were nothing. Feel it. Hanging around is good enough.

Choices

A lot of people look at non-duality and say, "But how do you make decisions?" Perhaps you don't. You just get to be chosen and you get chosen through. And every moment you are being chosen, even when you think you chose—you didn't choose—you were chosen—get out of it! This is from Dag Hammarskjöld's *Markings*:

Tired
And lonely,
So tired
The heart aches.
Meltwater trickles
Down the rocks,

---

[43] *Selected Poems of Rainer Maria Rilke*, trans. Robert Bly, Harper and Row, 1981 p. 199

Chapter 6: The Path of Non-Duality

The fingers are numb,
The knees tremble.
It is now,
Now, that you must not give in.
On the path of the others
Are resting places,
Places in the sun
Where they can meet.
But this
Is your path,
And it is now,
Now, that you must not fail.
Weep
If you can,
Weep,
But do not complain.
The way chose you --
And you must be thankful.[44]

Age

You could also age gracefully. I run by a ninety year-old woman's house every day. She is out there every day with a greeting; and she is all wrinkled up; and she is very gray; and she is quite stooped; and she has done no plastic surgery, but

---

[44] Dag Hammarskjöld, <u>Markings</u>, 1961: 12, 213 (dated 6 July 1961)

she is an inspiration as she ages gracefully!... So is my mother; so is my little dog.

Stand for Something

You could stand for something. You could sing your own song whether it's pretty or not. You could be a Corazano Aquino in the Philippines who lost the election; you could be a mother in a home raising a child—nobody will write about you. You could just stand for something—which does not have to be against anything.

Meaning

It is believed non-duality implies life has no meaning; no caring. The truth is meaning becomes infinite. It is every instant—it is the intensity of every instant, every instant, every walk of the foot, every move of the hand, not that it be right or wrong, but just that you have made the movement; taken the step in the instant. Friday evening I was driving to a wedding and a seagull was hurt, a broken wing, on the road unable to fly. (There I was, 'uncaring' they say?[45] On the

---

[45] Since the perception is that non-dualism has no priority, it is perceived to be uncaring. (Ed.)

Chapter 6: The Path of Non-Duality

contrary; the caring is even more intense because you are more present to be in the moment.) I stopped my car in the middle of traffic and like some kind of mad woman, who looked as if she cared a whole lot for this seagull, guided that seagull across the street and threw my beautiful $150 coat over it. I picked it up in my arms and took it to be cared for at the Alexander Lindsay Junior Museum. I was fully present, the self was gone, and everything had precious, awesome, and infinite meaning.

> *You see, I want a lot.*
> *Perhaps I want everything:*
> *the darkness that comes with every infinite fall*
> *and the shivering blaze of every step up.*
>
> *So many live on and want nothing*
> *and are raised to the rank of prince*
> *by the slippery ease of their light judgments.*
>
> *But what you love to see are faces*
> *that do work and feel thirst.*
> *You love most of all those who need you*
> *as they need a crowbar or a hoe.*
> *You have not grown old, and it is not too late*
> *to dive into your increasing depths*
> *where life calmly gives out its own secret.*[46]

---

[46] *Selected Poems of Rainer Maria Rilke*, p. 27

5: Enjoying the moment with Cindy and O'Keefe yawning

7: THE PATH OF MEDITATION

March 2, 1986

The Nature of Meditation

Meditation in the traditional and charismatic churches causes a lot of fear in people. There is a belief that somehow through the meditative process, one will bring in the 'devil' or spirits, or the presence of God will be invoked which might be dangerous. That is not how Unity sees it. Unity is a balance between Western and Eastern tradition. The founder of Unity, Charles Fillmore, studied Eastern traditions seriously and brought to Unity the practice of meditation. In fact, the symbol of the Unity wings[47] found on *Daily Word* literature, *Unity Magazine* and all Unity literature from Lee's Summit, Missouri came through his devotion to meditation. Those who knew him in his later years said that he lived in the meditative

---

[47] This symbol is no longer widely used in Unity's literature. Also known as the wings of Isis, this symbol is still found in many Unity churches. (Ed.)

presence full time. So, our position at Unity is that meditation is nothing to fear. We believe that through its practice one will have an internal experience with God and find that God is ever more present.

Connection with God

You do remember, don't you, that you are 'hooked-in' with the Infinite.

> *But when a man turns to the Lord the veil is removed. Now the Lord is the Spirit, and where the Spirit of the Lord is, there is freedom. And we all, with unveiled face, beholding the glory of the Lord, are being changed into his likeness from one degree of glory—to another; for this comes from the Lord who is the Spirit. (II Corinthians 3: 16-18)*

It is believed that through meditation one is capable of removing that veil. Epictetus stated:

> *You are a distinct portion of the essence of God and contain a certain part of Him in yourself. Why, then, are you ignorant of your noble birth? Why do you not consider whence you came? Why do you not remember, when you are eating, who you are who eat, and whom you feed?... Do you*

Chapter 7: The Path of Meditation

not know that it is the Divine you feed, the Divine you exercise? [48]

Consider this beautiful phrase from Paul, the man who, while on the road to Damascus, was struck by the movement of God within him and it changed his life. In a letter he writes these words:

I know a man in Christ who fourteen years ago was caught up to the third heaven [that is how he describes what his experience with meditation was like] whether in the body or out of the body, I do not know, but God knows. And I know that this man was caught into paradise, whether in the body or out of the body, I do not know, God knows. And that man heard things that cannot be told which man may not utter. On behalf of this man I will boast, but on my own behalf I will not boast, except in my weakness. Though through it I wish to boast I shall not be a fool or I shall be speaking the truth. But I refrain from it so that no one may think more of me than he sees in me or hears from me. [49]

He is describing his tremendous experience in touching his spiritual self. Here are more lines in

---

[48] Epictetus, *Discourses*, Thomas Wentworth Higginson, Ed., Book 2, pp 1134-1135

[49] I Corinthians 14

127

which he describes what one might experience in the meditative domain:

> *Now there are varieties of gifts, but the same Spirit; and there are varieties of service, but the same Lord; and there are varieties of working, but it is the same God who inspires them all in everyone. To each is given the manifestation of the Spirit for the common good. To one is given through the Spirit the utterance of wisdom, and to another the utterance of knowledge according to the same Spirit, to another faith by the same Spirit, to another the working of miracles, to another prophecy, to another the ability to distinguish between spirits, to another various kinds of tongues, to another the interpretation of tongues. All these are inspired by one and the same Spirit, who apportions to each one individually as he wills.*[50]

The Fruits of Meditation

Most of us wander around in the course of our daily existence thinking that we are only human. And there is nothing wrong with being only human as many of us need to be more fully human in many respects since a lot of us use our spirituality to escape our humanity. As you sit with yourself, remember that you are God. Remember that resting inside you is an eternal and

---

[50] I Corinthians 12: 4-11

Chapter 7: The Path of Meditation

internal, Infinite place wherein you can tap—where you can experience the fullness about which Paul is talking.

This week I saw a woman on television who is a healer here in the Bay Area—clearly she is so imbued with the presence of Spirit within that she freely and willingly shares to heal people. Have you thought recently about the fact that you are a healer? Have you gotten so absorbed in your everyday life of making money and doing your chores and taking care of your relationships that you have forgotten that you are a well and inside your well there is a gem to be discovered? Have you forgotten that inside you—you have recourse and the capacity to make contact with all the wisdom that is in the Universe? There is no reason to be blocked by creative issues; there is no reason to be blocked by not having enough ideas; there is no reason to be blocked by the possibility that even though you are the 'underdog', you have the capacity to express all of the potential that lies within you. Have you forgotten recently that you are in tune and one with the magnificent Christ Principle that heals you, prospers you, enflames you, empowers you and makes you far more than you believe you are? Have you been too caught in your physical body and your physical situation?

The Path of God

Throughout the ages mystics, teachers, religions, spiritual organizations have tried to awaken people to the recognition that they are not dull, they are not prosaic, they are not commonplace, they are not limited; and they are not held back by their brain, their mind, their education, their wherewithal, goods, or income. There is far more that resides way inside them, and there is a way for that "imprisoned splendor" as Robert Browning[51] called it to be released, to be tapped. The key to that is through the power of meditation. It annoys me that so many people 'hang around' and say, "Well, I guess God's going to get this venture done and I can just sit around," and then they feel miserable while they sit around. Well, it is clear that if you want to become involved in your spirituality you must find a way to unleash your potential. You don't just sit around and be passive about it. In this area of life you cannot be. Oh, yes, God is going to take care of the whole Universe—it is on its way—it is moving on to Omega point as Tielhard de Chardin stated. And you and I, if we want to assist in speeding up that process, can do that through meditation.

---

[51] Robert Browning was a Victorian Poet noted for dramatic phrases and word pairings. (Ed.)

Chapter 7: The Path of Meditation

There is an old story which I've told many times and it goes like this:

When God was designing the Universe, he/she knew that God wanted to create something that would be in His image-likeness and the creation was to have been each of us. The way this came into form was that God was sitting around on a Saturday evening with his drinking buddy. The two of them loved to play good jokes. On this particular evening God was saying, "I really want to bring this thing out of everywhere and put it into form."

And the buddy said, "What form?"

And God said, "Well, I think I'll call it planet Earth."

And the buddy said, "Well, I think that sounds like a good idea."

So they continued rapping for about a half hour. And then God said, "Well, I don't think 'earth' will be good enough, I think I would like to create somebody in my image. And that somebody will have a head, a body, some legs and arms and eyes, and it will have a brain and a form and a shape. And it will grow into maturity and gradually come to know its own being, and it will look and act, very much, like me—having all power."

And the buddy was really excited. Then the buddy said, "Is that all it is going to be? Are you going to tell this being everything?"

The Path of God

And God thought and thought and said, "No, I don't think I'll tell everything, I think I'll leave one piece out."

So the buddy said, "What's that?" And God replied, "Well, it will be about his real potential... I think I'll hide that from him. It will make life exciting."

So the buddy said, "Yes, but you're going to create this being in your image-likeness, right? Well, if you do, he'll certainly find it."

And God said, "No, we'll hide it someplace very special."

And the buddy said, "Where?"

And God said, "Well, what about in darkest Africa?"

The buddy said, "No, he'll certainly find that—he's very clever—very, very clever."

And then God said, "Well what about putting it atop the tallest tree in the Redwoods?"

And the buddy said, "Oh, no he'll certainly find that."

And then God said, "Yes, he certainly would. What about if I put it at the bottom of the deepest ocean—fathoms deep?"

And the buddy said, "Oh... no... surely he will find it there."

Chapter 7: The Path of Meditation

And then God had a light bulb experience. He said, "I know I'll put it inside him—he certainly won't think to look for it there."

And that is what happened. It got planted inside you and you and you and yet we have continued to think that God cannot be found. Lying inside of you, inside of me, is a gem, a diamond, and it shines. When you discover it, when you dare to catch it inside your hand, and when you dare to get close enough to it—to experience it, its power is stupendous. Inside of it are all the answers. In contacting it, one gains conviction and power; and when you touch it, you know you have touched what is called in the Unity movement—the Christ. When you touch it, it enflames you. Have you ever been out in the forest and felt lost and seen a spark of light flickering through the trees and something inside you woke-up and said, "Yes?" Have you fallen in love recently or can you remember when you did—and you saw in another human being something that felt like a spark or a diamond shone—and it shone for a brief minute and you responded? Have you heard a pop rock concert lately and seen a star up there who knew how to communicate with an audience and something inside you started radiating and you felt... yes? Well, that gem was touched in you that moment. The door in you was opened for a brief moment and it gave you a sense... yes... yes... there is something, something I forgot between the age of three and eight... something I used to cavort with between three and eight, but it closed down. And it is intended to close down so that we will seek to touch it again.

I have just shared that with as much drama as possible, to entice you to want to bother to go looking for it again. I don't share this very often, but you are looking at a woman who has touched it. I touched it the first time at the age of seventeen—it woke me in the middle of the night, and it healed my eyes for fifteen minutes—until it closed down again. I touched it again at thirty at Unity Ministerial School, and it opened me up for three months—I walked in ecstasy. And it touched me again in March 1979 when it implanted itself in my heart, and it has never left. I am here constantly to tell people, "Come, let's go look." If you want it, you can have it.

Commitment

And, if you want it, you must make a commitment. And that commitment must be total. You cannot give up the commitment because you got drunk one night and couldn't bother to pay attention. You can't give up the

Chapter 7: The Path of Meditation

commitment because your 'ship didn't come in'. You cannot give up the commitment because you happen to get sick or because your lover walked away. You cannot give up the commitment because you went bankrupt. You cannot give up the commitment because you fell in love and it all 'got easy again'.

Consider this Javanese story:

> *In Java they tell of a young blade, who spied a beautiful maiden on the high road and followed her deliberately for a mile. Finally, she wheeled and demanded, "Why do you dog my footsteps?" "Because," he declared fervently, "you are the loveliest thing I've ever seen and I have fallen madly in love with you at sight—be mine." "But, you have merely to look behind you," said the girl, "to see my young sister who is ten times more beautiful than I am." The gallant cavalier wheeled about and his gaze fell on as ugly a wench as ever drew breath in Java. "What mockery is this?" he demanded of the beautiful girl. "You lied to me." "So did you," she replied. "If you were so madly in love with me, why did you turn around?"*

Commitment: I was in Mt. Shasta yesterday to do the "Prayer of the Heart" workshop. People always ask me, when I do the "Prayer of the Heart" workshop, "Whatever made you make the commitment?" And I say simply, "There was nothing else to do." And they always say, "Well, what will the results be?" And my promise is: nothing… nothing. You don't enter in to the meditative life to get your life straight, to make it 'good', to make it work, to clean up your relationships, or to get healed. If that happens, that is a by-product. The commitment must be "Only to Thee, my Lord. Only through Thee will I seek the gem within." And when the gem is touched the gem awakens the Life. You can find those who have touched the gem in Calcutta, India; you can find those who have touched the gem in the ghettos of our country; you can find those who have touched the gem as millionaires atop huge corporations. Those who touch the gem understand—it has nothing to do with the external display or the external results—but they have touched the gem.

Touching the Gem Inside of You

And how do you touch the gem? There seem to be three simple truths about it.

Remove External Stimuli

The first is that you must remove all external stimuli. That is why the meditative practice is done consistently, day by day, in the same place, usually at the same time, where you sit in a quiet place and find some position that is comfortable

Chapter 7: The Path of Meditation

for you and there practice removing the stimulus. How do you remove the stimulus? Well, you relax in a chair; you turn off the telephone; you tell your friends, not to call you, you say to your kids, "I am going into my quiet place." And then you shut off the stimulus. Many people say, "Well, do I quiet the mind?" I don't really think so because I don't think you can quiet the mind. So, what do they do when they say, "Quiet the mind." All they mean is that you remove your attention from the external world and bring the attention within. That's all. Point number one.

Concentration

Point number two, concentration. You must know how to bring the attention inside and then concentrate and keep the concentration inside. And in the meditative experience at the end of this lesson on touching the gem you will practice this.

Go Deep

And third, deepen. Imagine just for a minute that in the meditative practice you are sending soundings way down into the depths of yourself until you experience some sounding that sounds like contact has been made with the gem. I have no other way to describe it. When I go into meditation, I go inside, and then find myself coming up, as if for a breath of air; and then at that moment I invite the sounding to go down inside, deeper. Usually, I use some kind of Christian terminology as I invite the Spirit to be revealed to me, and thus the sounding goes deeper. And then when it starts to come up again, invite it deeper.

People then ask questions, "And what happens inside?" "Do you hear words?"

...Sometimes.

"Do you see lights?"

...Sometimes.

"Do you see visions?"

...Sometimes.

"Do you see colors?"

...Sometimes.

"Do you get senses and feelings of knowing?"

...A lot of the time.

"Does God talk in big sounds and waves?"

Chapter 7: The Path of Meditation

...Usually not.

"Is it subtle?"

...Oh, yes and the more you do it, the more subtle it gets—more subtle—more subtle.

Meditative Practice

Now, let's stop and enter into a led meditative practice. Remember that we are going to seek a gem. Relax and get inside yourself. Be with yourself in your chair, quiet, and imagine that you are going on a wonderful journey, and I will do my best to help create that.

> *May I assume you are comfortable and that you are letting the chair hold you so that there is no separation between you and the chair? You are letting your breath lead you. You remember that there is a gem within you that you would like to touch. What you are doing right now has merit and it will take you where it takes you. Let your breath become the rhythm that deepens you. If you find yourself distracted, let yourself be distracted. The process itself will get your attention. So, don't fight—don't mind the wanderings. You can hear my voice; I will support you and guide you. But, keep breathing and keep following the breath. Attend to your breath. Become the rhythm of breathing deeply—more and more relaxed. Don't be afraid of going to sleep; just keep with the breathing. And I am breathing with you and we are becoming an entrained, breathing heart.*

Gradually let more of your attention move into the body so that any part of your body that feels tense or tight—you become aware of and assist it in relaxing. As you relax, you go deeper and deeper. Don't worry about your thought, just let it be what it is—don't fight. Be in your body. Now, have this awareness for a moment, "I have a body; I AM not only my body; [Pause] I have a body; I AM not only my body." [Pause] And then let the body slip into the background of consciousness.

No doubt now you are aware of lots of mind chatter. Continuing the breathing, let the mind chatter go on—it frankly doesn't really matter. Let it come and go like waves at a beach. Let it pass through like the water in a brook. And then consider this, "I have thoughts, and I AM not only my thoughts. [Pause] I see that I have thoughts, and I am not only my thoughts." [Pause] And then feel your mind move into the background as you go deeper with the attention.

And now, let's go deeper: concentration, attention… way inside where you know. Now just be with your attention way inside. If thought comes back or your body comes back, let it, but keep the attention going deeper maybe into the heart or into the third eye. [Pause]

And now I invite you to listen… listen to you beneath the mind… beneath the body. Don't try, don't push, wait! It is like seeing beneath the ocean. Every so often there will be a wisp of something that will come by that will seem incredibly unique. Watch… wait. [Long Silence].

Chapter 7: The Path of Meditation

Stay where you are and listen. [Long Silence].

Time requires as always that beginnings end. Our Western minds have thought that since it ends, it is finished. Where you have been is a beginning and it continues even though you bring your attention back to usual things. Whenever ending a meditation, take the seed of where you have been and consciously leave it planted to grow and somehow say inside yourself, "I'll be back. I'll be back to watch again. Trust me!" And somehow put your hands over the seed work you have done and give it a blessing, for it, like anything fresh and new, needs the warmth and support before you leave it.

Truth lies within us. It takes no rise from outward things.

Whatever you may believe, there is an inmost center within us all

Where Truth abides in fullness and around wall upon wall the gross flesh hems it in.

This perfect clear perception which is Truth

A baffling and perverting carnal mesh binds it.

And to know rather consists in opening out a way from whence the imprisoned splendor may escape

Than in affecting entry for a light supposed to be without.[52]

And that is meditation.

Gradually come back into this room and gradually open your eyes. As you do so—in quietness—remember where you have been and the seed that is growing; and somehow have some awareness of gently carrying that until you can come back to unleash the hidden splendor again. Promise yourselves that. Take a breath of air now—consciously, here in the room.

---

[52] Robert Browning, *Paracelsus* (Ed.)

8: THE PATH OF PRAYER

March 9, 1986

Introduction

This lesson is the most important lesson I could offer anyone desiring to develop their spirituality. The doctoral dissertation I wrote over a six-year period is entitled, *The Prayer of the Heart—A Method for Transformation.* As a result of the dissertation, which became a six-year experience, prayer has become a life process for me. So as I share this with you, realize that this is my life; this is my heart on the line.

Concepts of Prayer

Here is a comment from a Hasidic Priest from Judaism, "All that is important is rare. Millions and millions of people inhabit the earth, but only a few are Jewish. Among the Jews only a few are learned. Among the learned, only a few are pious. And even fewer are those who know how to pray properly."

The Path of God

Evangelist Billy Graham told a Richmond, Virginia audience that Elizabeth Taylor was more to be pitied than censured and suggested that his audience pray for her. From the back of the auditorium, a listener responded, "I've been praying for her for forty years and haven't got her yet!"

A new neighborhood newspaper called *Wisdom's Child*, published in Manhattan's upper West Side, ends by noting that life there can be a delightful thing. That said the editors offer a cut-out page of emergency telephone numbers for fireman, police, suicide prevention, addict assistance, a 24-hour locksmith, air pollution, a poison control number and dial-a-prayer. The recorded prayer, "Oh, Lord, I'm very aware I live in a world of muggers and purse-snatchers. I earnestly pray for help to keep my perspective. And even if I am a victim of a crime, I pray for those who have thus abused me."

Johnny was in his pajamas and mother was hearing his bedtime prayers. And, "Please God," he was saying, "Let Daddy give me that electric train for Christmas and have the teacher notice how much better I am doing now and make the big kids take me into their gang and… " Suddenly, the mother interrupted, "Don't take it on yourself

Chapter 8: The Path of Prayer

to give God instruction; just report for duty." (That doesn't have to be told to a child, does it?)

J. Edgar Hoover, former FBI head, stated, "The spectacle of a nation praying is more awe-inspiring than the explosion of an atomic bomb. The force of prayer is greater than the possible combination of man-made or man-controlled powers, because prayer is man's greatest means of trapping the Infinite resources of God."

This prayer was noted by an abbot, "I don't ask for an immediate response, Lord, all I want is a commitment."

A minister was heard to say once, "I'm not going to say Amen. The way things have been going, we better keep in touch." [Carol Ruth often interjected humor, occasionally from clips sent to her by her mother, to lighten the tone of her messages. (Ed.)]

Prayer—A Connection

This was stated by Bishop W. Appleton Lawrence, "If God knows what we want and wills to give what is best for us, what is the use of praying at all? The very asking of this question shows a fundamental, failure to understand the purpose of prayer. The object of prayer is not to

The Path of God

inform God or correct God's plan, to drag His wisdom down to our intelligence, but rather to educate us into more intimate personal relationships with God."

Our tendency has been, in our growing up with prayer, to think that we are that little boy who keeps ordering God what to do, thereby putting God outside, and to think that somehow we can bring God down to our level. And as we mature in prayer and in our spiritual life, we have to expand our prayer attitudes and look at them in a whole different way—at least that is what I had to do. Let me give you three simple experiences that might help you take another look at prayer than thinking it is cajoling or begging or asking or demanding or criticizing or visualizing or expecting or hoping.

Recently I bought a big screen television. When it was brought out to be hooked-up, the hook-up was not performed accurately at all. For about two and a half weeks I have been annoyed because I cannot get what I want on the television screen. Listen to those words: I can't get what I want on the television screen... think about that—we can't get what we want on our inner television screens. So, yesterday morning I was up at 6 a.m. because I wanted to record *Starman* on HBO. I have a big

Chapter 8: The Path of Prayer

box of TV stuff such as extraneous TV plugs and wires. I believed I could figure out a way to make the TV work. I put the AB switch back on, connected up all kinds of wires and jacks. I was very serious, very committed, and very devoted. So after fiddling and fuddling with the 'thing' for an hour, and yet it still was not hooked up as I wanted it to be, and it was not working correctly. So I left it the way it was and recorded *Starman*.

At 10:30 a.m. I called the store that was responsible for hooking up the TV incorrectly. I 'screamed and yelled' over the phone with the best communication skills that I know.

The manager listened and said, "I know what's wrong, do this and do this, do this, and do this, and then go ahead and try it and call me back."

So, I went upstairs and did this, and this and this, and it still didn't make any difference, so I called him back. He didn't know what to do with it, so I called Viacom. (I know this is a long story, but it is all very important!)

When I called Viacom, the lady said, "Oh, I know what it is. Take out a piece of paper and draw a diagram." I figured that by now I was really talking to someone who could communicate. So, she said, "Do this, do this, and do this." I drew it

The Path of God

all on a piece of paper, went upstairs and did all that I was supposed to do—and it still didn't work.

Tomorrow evening a professional TV 'hooker-upper' is going to be at my house to hook up that TV the way it needs to be hooked-up. But, the point of this story is this: you can have all of the external information you want or need; you can have all the right equipment; you can have all the right jacks, ropes, pieces of wire, pictures on a piece of paper—but if somewhere inside you—you don't have that connecting link that will join you with the Truth about it all and give you the vital information that puts it into synchronicity, it doesn't connect! You see, we can hang around; we can go to all the EST courses; we can go to all the Unity seminars: we can listen to all the ways to make our life work; take relationship seminars, learn how to fair-fight, do primal scream, affirm your way in and out of hell and deny it; you can think the right thoughts; you can clean up your internal life, and you still may not be able to make it work because you are working with the externals out there... and the missing link is the connector that will connect you to that Something that is God. You don't tell God what to do; somehow you find a system that will allow you to

Chapter 8: The Path of Prayer

put yourself in front of God and show up for instruction.

Here is a similar story. I bought a computer about a year ago. I played with it all summer and did a pretty good job with it. But this winter I am taking a course in computers. I talked to a man in Stockton yesterday; he bought a computer two years ago and still cannot make it work! Why? Because there is no connecting link there that bonds him with the total basis of information that allows him to make the computer work.

[At this point Dr. Knox sits down and plays a portion of the *Fantaisie Impromptu* by Chopin. She plays it easily and fluidly. Then she plays it again as she first learned it. It is designed as a musical work which places six notes in the left hand against four notes in the right hand. It is stilted and obvious, slow moving—it is one of the most difficult skills to 'bring together' in music. She then plays it again, fluidly, easily revealing the capacity to move from the stilted into the fluid.]

The question arises as to how a person can get from the stilted to the fluid. It is accomplished by spending hours sitting at the piano with the difficult and tedious beginnings until a connection is found which finally releases the performer from the profane into the Divine: the profane is the limits, the impossibility, the difficulty, and thinking you know how to do it, only to step into that place where something suddenly clicks and you are released and you transcend. In terms of the spiritual life, the analogous skill is prayer... it is the connector carrying us into transcendence.

We can see this analogy in so many different expressions. Haven't you tried to 'right think' your way to God in prayer; haven't you prayed when life wasn't good and forgot about praying when life was good? Haven't you tried visualization, tried to get rid of judgments, and tried to forgive? Those are the wires and connectors, the computer keyboard, the piano keys and musical notes. Yet they don't get us to the Essence, to the inner knowledge—the power source. The prayer that is the channel—the funnel that connects us with the larger piece of pie—is not a series of gadgets and externals but something far simpler, far more profound!

Plotinus states, "Let us know God Himself, not in mere form of words, but by elevating our souls to Him in prayer. And the only way, truly to pray is to approach alone the one that is alone. To contemplate that one, we must withdraw into the inner soul as into a temple and there be still." You

Chapter 8: The Path of Prayer

see, the point with prayer, and the one that I have tried to convey through these three examples, is that prayer is actually finding a way to extend our antenna into a whole other level of experience than the one we know. And the way we have tried to pray has been to keep 'tuning' the radio into the present channel. As long as one keeps on tuning into the present channel, which is my needs, my wants, my hopes, my agonies, my problems, even though those are a clearing house, he/she remains tuned into the same channel.

The art of prayer—the one that I had to struggle to come to terms with—is the art that realizes I am seeking to send an antenna into zones I have never traveled before. As I practice extending this antenna through prayer, I/you can walk this earth, moving into those zones and touching into them, giving another channel of receptivity. I believe that is why I am given the gift of creativity. I believe that is the reason I am given the gifts of continuing to be able to love. That is why I am given the gifts of continually being able to be here now. I don't talk about just me alone—I am talking about any 'I'—the 'I' isn't just the Carol Knox 'I', it is the 'I' of all of us. And if we take prayer out of the commonplace, out of the banal, and out of the 'what is' and shove it into the 'what has the potential for me to capture and express',—like an antenna hanging extended out there, hanging round able to catch what the Universe sends through for me to pick up and to bring in—then prayer becomes the connector. But most of us pray saying, "This is what I want; this is what I need; this is what I think we should have; this is the way we should raise the money; this is the way the service should go; this is the way so-and-so should act; this is how the relationship should be; this is how I am going to manifest my hope for retirement." Then you perpetuate the same channel... the extension is lost, and banality and closure sets in.

In Romans 8:1, Paul says this: "For the law of the Spirit of life in Christ Jesus has set me free from the law of sin and death." He is talking about that antenna. Spirit has the capacity to override or supersede the lower laws—and that does not mean they are bad or less—but they just are lower laws of the mental and physical plane.

Consider this poem from Kabir:

> *Between the conscious and the unconscious,*
> *The mind has put up a swing:*
> *All earth creatures, even the supernovas,*
> *Sway between these two trees,*
> *And it never winds down.*

Chapter 8: The Path of Prayer

We are always hungering to transcend, to ascend, that is built into us. And as we hunger, so we are reached for. As we hunger, our being is pulled toward. I call it the great push/pull of the universe. The push/pull here on earth is a pushing away and pulling toward causing us to feel stretched. But in the spiritual life the push/pull works together. Thus Kabir's comment that the swing sways and it never winds down it is always working in you—your hunger, in a way, is your prayer. More of Kabir's poem:

> *Angels, animals, humans, insects by the million,*
> *Also the wheeling sun and moon;*
> *Ages go by, and it goes on.*
> *Everything is swinging: heaven, earth, water, fire,*
> *And the secret one slowly growing a body.*

And what is the body? The body is the expanded consciousness. And now the concluding line of the poem:

> *Kabir saw that for fifteen seconds and it made him a servant for life.*[53]

---

[53] *The Kabir Book*, Robert Bly, (Beacon Press 1977) p. 11

I saw it for fifteen minutes in March of 1979 and it took over my life's intention and dedication forever—and my way to there was prayer; prayer without hope, without expectation—just to be a prayer.

How Shall We Pray?

Well, if all this is true about prayer—if I have caught your attention—then how shall we pray? It is so simple! I would like to read a quote from Gandhi.

> *It is better to have a heart without words than words without a heart. Prayer is no flight of eloquence; it is no lip homage. It springs from the heart. If, therefore, we achieve that purity of the heart when it is emptied of all but love, if we keep all the chords in proper tune, they tumble past in music and out of sight. Prayer needs no speech. It is in itself independent of any sensuous effort. I have not the slightest doubt that prayer is an unfailing means of cleansing the heart of pollution. But it must be combined with the utmost humility.*

We wonder how a person like Gandhi kept carrying this vision—there is the reason! So what is required in order that we pray?

Chapter 8: The Path of Prayer

The Open Heart

Well, we must bring ourselves to the altar with an open heart. I would like to share with you once again the closing of the film, *Places in the Heart*. In that movie, at the very end, after we have watched a family torn by all kinds of difficulties: a man killed by a black man; a black man who has saved a woman beaten up by the Ku Klux Klan having to leave what he loves; the situations of having no money; a person struggling to make it day by day; an affair—these are all our issues! Yet, at the very end, while the performers are sitting in a church service, Holy Communion is passed. And as the communion plate is passed, the viewer realizes that everybody has gathered together, including those who have been killed or mistreated. As the viewer watches this closing scene, all of them are reaching out to touch, to connect, and to bond beyond the misdemeanors of life—through communion, their hearts are opened! The heart, open, beyond ego, has become malleable and porous! An open heart is the inner attitude of kneeling—Gandhi says it must be humble. And as you kneel, you must open yourself up and let go of everything that you would carry-in based on your expectations, your hopes, your angers, your revenges, and your resentments—because in prayer they do not belong. They have to be left outside the gate as you walk inside to the altar, and recline yourself there, the words are, "Here I am, accept and love me as I am. I will open my heart for something new, for new attitudes, a new way of being, a new connection, a new understanding. Here I am, Lord." That is the open heart—the ego has to be left outside. And when the ego is left outside the door, the heart naturally breaks. Prayer, in the spiritual life, is 'about the heart breaking' business.

Keeping the Attention Within

The second aspect of prayer is that you must be willing to keep a portion of you there. As I walk the earth—and many of you know this—the basic commitment is to keep your attention with God 24 hours a day, if at all possible. And there is a way to do this. (I can't give it to you here in a Sunday morning lesson, but I can teach you how to do it if you will be with me in the "Prayer of the Heart" workshop). The requirement of ongoing prayer, the requirement of mature prayer, the requirement of spiritual prayer, (the prayer I am presenting in this lesson), and the requirement of prayer that goes beyond conditions, terms, expectations, hopes, desires, and one's limited sense of one's self, is that you must put yourself before the altar full time. It is this request that

Chapter 8: The Path of Prayer

people tend to disconnect from me, and it is my greatest sadness. They disconnect from me because somehow they think I am not serious. They think that this request is impossible. Yet, you are looking at a woman who brings heart into the presence of God 24 hours a day. The way I do this is by simply keeping my attention in the heart. And you can do it this instant. And if you make it a lifetime practice, it becomes the channel that connects you with the underground. The 'mind-blowing' reality about my dissertation was that it was so simple... don't we always say that about Truth—it is so simple? The simplicity is to bring your heart before God full time and then practice spiritual prayer—if you want to be a monastic walking the earth rather than stuck in a cloister.

Consider yourself this minute as you put your attention in your heart. The key is that if you would get rid of the bitterness, the burdens, the barriers... then you must keep your heart, your being, in front of the flame of the Spirit full time, so that it might warm it all! We are not all warm, are we? We have a lot of calluses, a lot of breaches, a lot of differences, a lot of walls, and a lot of barriers. The call for spiritual prayer is to bring your heart before the flame and leave it there—no matter what you are doing—leave it there. So when you are gardening, when you are cooking your dinner, when you are making love, or when you are watching television, keep yourself before the flame in the heart. Leave your heart there. People talk about this being the age of the heart. I wonder if they realize that the age of the heart has nothing to do with being good, or being kind, or compassionate, or friendly, that is solar plexus development, not the heart. That must be developed first; then it is time for the heart. The heart is a much richer vehicle; it has to do with opening and non-resistance and letting go and breaking up inside to become pliant, malleable, open, porous, and available—vehicular—for God.

The Rhythm

And then the third part of this is so difficult to describe because if you have studied anything professionally, you know all about this. And remember, prayer is a professional way of life—it is an attitude of life. It isn't looking good in public; it isn't being a 'saint'. Prayer is an inner attitude. It is the vehicle for your life, for every life in this room, for every life the world over (and far more of them are practicing this than us Christians in the Western world... that is what my travels have shown me). You know that if you want to do anything professional, it is a requirement that you must do it and do it and do

Chapter 8: The Path of Prayer

it and do it and do it until the 'thing' becomes automatic. It becomes a rhythm, and once you do it and do it (in prayer the doing is pay attention... pay attention... pay attention), gradually something profound happens. It happens in every area of life—it happens in sports, it happens in artistry, it happens in dance or playing the piano—finally the rhythm 'gets you' and when that happens, then the prayer prays you and you become a prayer.

So the runner runs and runs and runs every day. And one day he is running and all of a sudden the ground goes out from underneath his feet, and his body is no longer a limit. He cracks through the shell of the body and through the limits of gravity and he becomes the run. Larry Bird throws basketballs that way. Sometimes you will see him playing, and he will get into a rhythm, and it is his practice that has allowed him to enter into it. He goes on a 'roll' where he can't miss a basket. Most of us think that we can just get out there and throw and then never miss a basket. Yet the rhythm of consistency allows the freedom to take place—so it is in prayer!

Bring your heart to the altar. Let it be opened there. Leave it there constantly and put yourself there under all conditions. And practice the rhythm. Then one day the rhythm will take you over.

[At this point Dr. Knox plays the *Fantaisie Impromptu* in its stilted, difficult form. She continues playing, slowly moving it into greater and greater freedom until finally it is fluid, easy—the rhythm of presence has taken her/it over.]

To close, consider this quotation by Catherine de Hueck Doherty[54] about Catherine of Genoa[55]:

> *People begin to pray vocally and then later they go on to meditation and contemplation. Eventually they cease to pray because they become prayer.*

It captured them!

---

[54] She was known as Catherine Doherty Servant of God. She was a Roman Catholic social worker and renowned speaker. (Ed.)

[55] Saint Catherine of Genoa was a Roman Catholic mystic that served the sick and the poor. She was known to have lived in a state of constant connection with the Divine that occurred through years of fervent prayer. (Ed.)

Chapter 8: The Path of Prayer

*6: Music is an analogy for Prayer and Life:
transition from stilted to fluid freedom
(Carol Ruth Knox as a teenager playing the piano.)*

9: THE PATH OF THE HEART

March 16, 1986

Introduction

The heart is very important to me. It has been a rather shocking experience to discover what it truly is—and until I studied and wrote my dissertation—I had not really known what the heart was. I think I was like a lot of people; I thought the heart had to do with kindness, being gentle, compassionate and treating people decently. I had been committed to that kind of life experience; I had set myself up to act out a certain kind of behavior thinking that was 'heart business'. In today's new thought teachings, we are told we are in the "age of the heart", but I am not sure all of us really understand what the "age of the heart" is. I happen to be one of those who know what the 'heart business' is about, for I have spent the last eight years of my life with my attention in the heart as a way of opening my heart. I would like to share that with you through this lesson.

Indicators of a Hungering Heart

Do you ever feel barren? Do you sometimes experience overwhelming feelings of bitterness, bondage; do you find yourself bickering a lot, feeling bored with life? Do you occasionally feel as if you are on the inside of a cave, the cave feels gray, and you don't know how to get through the walls of that inner cave? Do you wake sometimes in the morning and lack a feeling of zest for life? You may have slept ten hours, but you are not at all renewed; the primary consciousness moving through the top of your head is a consciousness about relationships that have not treated you right, living situations that don't work, a kind of general feeling like a low-grade headache, which is a way of being? Does that touch any of you? You may be married to the 'perfect person'; you may have a wonderful job; you may have worked many different systems; tried to think right and even think 'wrong' and even that didn't work; you may have done a number of different workshops, and what you thought were 'openings' were not; only to have the 'thing' close down on you and then find that you feel even worse because you experienced a 'taste of honey'. But you didn't know how to keep the honey, so you return to the same 'buzz of consciousness' which is like a drone. Only it isn't the great Om of the Hindus, it

Chapter 9: The Path of the Heart

is just a 'here I am' again and I did not break through the cave.

I think that Unity does an excellent job of leading us to feel comfortable with it's being all right to be as we are—that there is nothing wrong with anger; there is nothing wrong with inner hunger; there is nothing wrong with passion or love or lust or jealousy or anxiety. I think we have been taught really well to find a way to trust that part of God's process within. Yet, the phenomenal perfectness of God's working within us is that God does not leave us alone. And even though we accept our general state of being, there is some urge within that says, "And I know I have a potential for beauty, expression, existence, life, loving, as a way of being in the world, and I am not tapping into it." Right? You know that you can accept yourself for all you are and yet, there is a stronger urge, a driving power within. The way it works is to keep pushing on the insides of your present state of consciousness. As it pushes, it tends to create greater disparity. Usually we tend to project the disparity upon our relationships, our working situations and our general environment. As we project it onto others, we are actually trying to push out the walls of our consciousness so that we can let in more light, so that we can try to be touched again by a memory that lives in our existence of a potential way of being.

As a part of this expanding process, an analogy may be made to our continuing to live inside of eggs—inside of eggs—inside of eggs. The process of life is that once you find yourself completed inside of a state consciousness or existence (an egg) you find that no longer satisfies you so there is a push on the edges of that limit. The minute the push begins, and you are able to extend your way through, you stretch the sides of the egg to create porous holes whereby you might move through and enter into a whole new space. Once there, you relax and say, "Ahhh... ," only to discover that the minute you said "Ahhh... ," you become a part of a bigger egg in which you exist causing the pressure mechanism to work its way out again. Let me remind you again that the way the pressure shows itself is through our projections on uncomfortable relationships, nagging personalities, financial situations, job experiences and anything else we can mention. But the process keeps moving on, changing, stretching.

I believe what is occurring within is: a huge portion of our existence is saying, "I want to leap from one way of existence into another way of

Chapter 9: The Path of the Heart

existence, and I wish there were a connecting link." The connecting link I discovered that was missing in my life was I had not yet entered into my heart. I entered into my heart clearly in March of 1979 after two years of devoted work with the Prayer of the Heart. The day I entered, I knew I had made a shift to another level of transcendence and ever since that moment I have stayed in that level of transcendence. Always, of course, wondering whether and when I will be kicked into another level.

To clarify this, we all know that in the Hindu system of the Eastern tradition there are seven chakras. The first one is known as the root chakra, located at the base of the spine, and it deals with our primal drives. Most of us involved at this [chakra] center have to spend much of our lives involved in primal drives. The second chakra is called the sexual chakra, and it deals with basic aggression and competitive drives that push us out into the world. There is nothing wrong with either of these two chakras—they must be satisfied. The third chakra is the solar plexus chakra which deals with our feeling nature, our passions, our hopes, our dreams, our fantasies, our ups and downs, our angers, etc. And we have all kinds of teaching mechanisms and explanations for those. Then we step into the fourth chakra which is the heart chakra. Interesting that it should be in the middle of our existence and that Ram Dass calls it the first step into transcendence. What does he mean by transcendence? It does not mean that you suddenly lop off the lower three chakras. Most religious teachings suggest lopping that part of us off, disconnecting from it, and carrying on. That is not the teaching at this center—the teaching is that you work with these until the indicators send you searching to move into the heart as a basic place from which to operate in the world. After the heart, incidentally, follows the throat chakra, the pineal gland chakra, and then the pituitary or crown chakra. When all of those chakras are open and free flowing, the system is believed to operate like a harmonizing flow, integrated with the world in which it operates and works.

I share that information with you to make something very obvious. A lot of teaching concerning the heart is confusing. I wouldn't believe I had the authority to talk about this, until I had devoted eight years of my life studying and researching the spiritual heart through the great saints and spiritual teachers over the past two thousand years. We have been very confused about what it means to be in the heart. As mentioned earlier, many of us have thought that

Chapter 9: The Path of the Heart

'heart' meant coming from niceness and kindness. The truth about studies of the heart, spiritually, is that the heart has to do with an energy; it has to do with a flame; it has to do with knowing how to excite that flame; how to stimulate and empower that flame, so that the flame takes over the activity and movement and direction of the life. Through its activity, it then incorporates the whole system and becomes the purifier, the refiner and the grower of the whole system—so that you give up responsibility and allow it to become the worker and the seeker and the urger. When this is completed, it is as if a flame has been lit in oil and then set onto the water of life. As the water of life moves up, our usual tendency is to move up with it, and as it moves down, so we do. But this flame, once lit, rather than losing oneself in the ascending and descending, burns slowly and smoothly through the whole experience. This flame releases conditions, duality, terms, and expectations with regard to life. It is a profound state, and it is the nature of transcendence. Transcendence is not killing the lower for the sake of the higher. It is confirming that the transcendent part—the flame in the heart—knows how to ride with the whole process without thinking that it should be any other way than the way it is—because the way it is—is Perfect.

Experiences with Touching the Heart

Here are a few key experiences and examples of how the heart functions when it is discovered. Before sharing these, as a point of clarification, sometimes when the heart is opened there is an emotional response. But the heart opening is not opening the emotion; it is opening a door into a state of being that lives in spite of life. Now to the first example, it comes from my dissertation entitled, *The Prayer of the Heart—A Method for Transformation*. Julian of Norwich, a medieval saint, was an amazing woman, and this is how she describes her discovery of the heart. She describes the sense of being immersed in the heart as a vision she had "where a little thing, the size of a hazelnut, was placed in her hand."[56] (Imagine that you have been seeking and through a prayerful state, somebody comes to you and places in your hand a "little thing the size of a hazelnut".) She continues. "As she looked at it, she wondered what it was and the answer came, 'it is all that is made'."[57] Now, the heart is the all that is made. It

---

[56] Carol Ruth Knox, *The Prayer of the Heart - A Method of Transformation*, p. 145

[57] Knox, *The Prayer of the Heart*, pp. 148-149

Chapter 9: The Path of the Heart

is the only truly important essence of your existence. It doesn't mean that the rest of your existence isn't important—the rest of your existence is the vehicle for the heart to be carried and captivated in the world. If you don't know its presence then you live as if it were not present, and you feel blocked, barren, bored, barricaded. So the message came to her, "it is all that is made."

Once again, she wondered how long it would last, for it was so small it looked as if it might fade away to nothing. Again the answer came, "it lasts and ever shall last for God loveth it and even so hath everything being—by the love of God." In this vision she observed three properties: one, that God made it; second; that God loves it; third, that God keeps it. How many of you know that? God made you, God loves you, and God keeps you. When you enter the heart and find a way to enflame it, you will know that God made all of you—what you call your sins and your strengths, your body as it is, your loves, your passions, your jealousies, your angers, your hopes, your dreams—all of you. Then you will know that God loves all of you. We must know that. If we live in the heart, we let go finally of any thought that there is any part that is unlovable. Yes, you are totally lovable! God loves totally without condition.

Through that, we see that God keeps us. In an age when we are all seeking to become responsible (and many of us have become over-responsible), we think we are supposed to keep this 'life' going, and that we even know how it should go, what will prove its going, and what the results will be when we connect with God. This teaching of the heart, as shown by Julian of Norwich, says something far more profound which when absorbed gives freedom: it says God keeps you. In 1979, I stopped bothering to figure-out most of life, bothering to try to discern what I should get rid of next. One evening while sitting in a hot tub, I asked the question, "Who is going to tell me what to do next in terms of what is right and wrong?" And the answer came, "I will." And it was my heart.

All last evening I sat with myself trying to find some image that I could give you that would communicate what the true heart is. All I could see was what I see inside and I would like to share it with you. I see that this hazelnut, this heart, is inside absolutely everybody... it is a hovering essence. That hovering essence probably rests in or near the heart, and it is hungering to be

Chapter 9: The Path of the Heart

touched. And it knows that you can touch it for yourself. Now obviously, some Sunday mornings I may touch it, or you may go to a musical concert, or fall in love and that outside person will have touched it. You will then give all of those externals responsibility for that awakening, opening, touching—but you will have forgotten that this occurrence is this moving, malleable, oozing, loving part of you that was touched. And if any individual merely bothers to bring his/her attention within, the essence moves out; and if you give it a little more attention it reaches out and you feel as if you embrace the world and nobody is barred from you, there are no walls. There are fears and angers and all that 'stuff', but there are no walls because the heart has opened. That is the hazelnut. And we must all remember here week after week, day after day, it is yours. And when you touch it you see your beauty and your possibility and you will know and dare to say, "I am God." And those words won't frighten you. You will expand out of the aquarium that has become too small for you and experience what a big 'fish' you really are. All I ever do all day, every day, around the world, is to remind you and hope to God it will take!

In the last lesson, at the piano, I played the first part of the *Fantaisie Impromptu* by Chopin. In this lesson, I will use the middle section of the work to show my best medium for what touching the heart is all about. First I will play it without heart—so to say. [As Dr. Knox plays, it is obvious the music is accurate, there is some feeling, and the expression and execution are well carried out. After finishing, she continues verbally.] We all hear a lot of people play the piano like that—play life like that—it is all right. Many people would give anything to play like that. Many of us get through life kind of idly, and it's adequate but we know, inside, there is always something missing.

Now, as I play this the second time, notice that I obviously go inside and when I do, I can assure you, I am touching my own heart. The way I do that—and I think I did this from a very young age without even knowing it—is to bring my attention down into my heart, where I live. I trust that there I tap into my search for and love of beauty—which is life's essence. We are all seeking beauty—we all know that potential, the heart, the power for exquisiteness, and beauty—and whenever we see it we know we are 'on'. [Dr. Knox plays the same work again, as described and the difference in intention and love inwardly can be seen. At the conclusion, Dr. Knox turns to the audience with these comments] It touched you—it got to you, didn't it? I went to my heart and I found you.

Chapter 9: The Path of the Heart

That is how we connect—through the heart, not even words, not even motions, not even sexual orgasms can make that kind of contact.

In the movie, *E.T. the Extra-Terrestrial* we were all moved to tears because we saw E.T.'s heart-light go out and we all wanted to be sure it did not go out—for that was ours! In the movie *Cocoon*, we saw the cocoons taken out of the water of support—and we watched a portion of our heart nearly die—and it caused our tears of loss. It is a universal knowing, this heart business—a flame, a power, an essence, and an energy, that hungers to be 'on', to be enflamed.

How Does One Touch The Heart?

How do you touch your heart? ...Not through the emotions, not through sexuality, and not through the primal part (none of which are 'bad' or out of order). But how—when you find yourself fed up with that mid-range of life—how do we move it on via the heart? Well, first you must know that there is a heart waiting in you—and you—and you. There is a heart lying in you hungering and wanting your attention. It often feels left-out. You will know it is most left-out when you find yourself bitching, bickering, banging on the inside of your head, and barricaded. All those symptoms are ever saying is, "Please come find me,"—it is waiting. It is like 'silly putty' [malleable and needing your first move]. You send it a knowing and it will spark and you will feel enflamed as you tend to it more and more.

To support this, I would like to read to you how the saints who have studied this for over 2,000 years have come to touch it. The following quotation is from Theophan the Recluse, a Russian monastic, who, in the late 19th century, began to bring to the surface studies of this 2,000 year old practice, and thereby brought it to the attention of the public. Pay attention because this is how your practice works. He says:

> *Feeling towards God—even without words—is a prayer. Guard this gift of feeling, given to you by the mercy of God. [This is nineteenth century English, so be careful of it.] How? First and foremost by humility, ascribing everything to grace and nothing to yourself. Secondly, dwell in grace and do not turn your heart or thought to anything else except necessity. Be all the time with the Lord. [And I am pointing to my heart.] If the inner flame begins to die down a little, immediately hasten to restore its strength [by bringing the attention into the heart].*[58]

---

[58] Knox, *The Prayer of the Heart*, pp. 148-149

Chapter 9: The Path of the Heart

And now this,

> To kindle in this heart such a divine love, to unite with God in inseparable union of love, it is necessary for a man to pray often, raising the mind to Him. For as a flame increases when it is constantly fed, so prayer, made often, with the mind dwelling ever more deeply in God, arouses divine love in the heart. And the heart, set on fire, will warm all the inner man, will enlighten and teach him, revealing to him all its unknown and hidden wisdom, and making him like a flaming seraph, always standing before God within his spirit, always looking at Him within his mind, and drawing from this vision the sweetness of spiritual joy.[59]

There is such a difference between spiritual joy and the usual joy versus sorrow—such a difference. It is heart business. And then this quotation:

> Fire in the heart may be kindled by ascetic striving, but such effort alone will not quickly kindle it into flame. There are many obstacles on the path. Therefore from ancient times those who were zealous... and experienced in the spiritual life... discovered another way to warm the heart... stand with your mind and attention in the heart,

---

[59] Knox, *The Prayer of the Heart*, p. 149

> *being very sure that the Lord is near and listening, and call to Him with fervor. ...Do this constantly. ...This will be exactly like holding an object in the sun, because this is to hold yourself before the face of the Lord. ...When this is performed with zeal, without laziness or omission, the Lord will... kindle the flame in your heart; and this flame is a sure testimony to the quickening of spiritual life in the innermost parts of your being, to the enthronement of the Lord within.*[60]

Zealous... without omission... constancy.

> *Desire to be filled with the Spirit, and sing with that aim in mind. Singing will set alight the Spirit or lead to a state of infusion by the Spirit or show forth His action... That is to say by singing with the tongue in the heart.*[61]

Conclusion

Now, I am hoping that as you have been reading, you have found more and more of your attention has been in the heart. It will not begin today. After two years of devotion, my heart opened. The day it opens, you will know. The day it opens, it will not be able to be closed. It never closes

---

[60] Knox, *The Prayer of the Heart*, p. 150

[61] Knox, *The Prayer of the Heart*, p. 154

again. You may have dryness, you may still bicker, but you have something more profound that continues to live in spite of life itself.

Now Where Does This Lead?

It leads to a state which I would like to describe as being like the French word, *le coeur*—heart — which formed our word courage. *Le Coeur*—courage—is the business of the heart. What is the state of the open heart? "It is the heart that loves God without any 'for'." Most of us love God for the results, for feeling good, for having a good relationship, for taking us where we want to go, for giving us sexual stimulus, and for offering us the gifts of the external world. Well, the heart business is a business that is beyond any 'for'. There is no reason that you love God—you just love God because it is the only way you can be any more.

> *It is the loving state beyond conditions or proof, without the dualist's demands for the good, without deadline or definition. It is the heart of no conditions; there are no conditions upon which love of self, love of others, love of the conditions themselves is based. It is unconditional love, the transcendent state. It is the person who has given up all without giving up the dance of life itself; and yet that person*

> *has given up nothing as he/she holds totally to God without requirement or even understanding all that it involves.*[62]

And finally, it leads to this: and who is the person with the open heart? How does this one live, what is the matrix of this being? The matrix is absolute courage. It is the faith that lives in the midst of fear and hope; it is a faith beyond duality, maybe even beyond God.

> *He hath heart who knoweth fear but vanquisheth it; who seeth the abyss, but with pride. He who seeth the abyss but with eagle's eyes, he who with the eagle's talons graspeth the abyss; he hath courage.*[63]

This is Abraham walking with his son to the altar without question or doubt—he has an open heart. This is Jesus riding into Jerusalem on Palm Sunday. And what is the courage, the heart of man? Well, he has done his work. He knows he is in God's hands and he goes forward without question. And finally, it is that image I used earlier: where each of you enflames the oil within your being and lighting the fire, you can set it

---

[62] Knox, *The Prayer of the Heart*, p. 154

[63] Frederich Wilhelm Nietzsche, *Thus Spake Zarathustra: A Book For All And None,* Ch. LXIII, The Higher Man

Chapter 9: The Path of the Heart

onto the ocean of life. The fire rides the ocean as it rises and falls, but you, with knowing, carry on with some sense of allness that supersedes and transcends the external world. And that is the path of the heart.

7: Carol Ruth Engaged in 'Heart Business'

The Path of God

10: THE PATH OF NON-RESISTANCE

March 23, 1986

Introduction

Before I begin this lesson, I would like to make it clear that 'non-resistance' is not the easiest idea to communicate—it is a frightening idea. Just this week I received a letter of anger complaining that my ministry was a ministry that teaches a lax morality and way of living, a "license to do whatever you like". That is often how non-resistance is interpreted—"license to do whatever you like". Frankly, that is not the nature of my own or Unity's devotion, and I hope to clarify the difference in this lesson. The material is important for clarification spiritually, so read it carefully, please.

Palm Sunday

In looking at Palm Sunday in the Unity philosophy, our belief is that Jesus enters into a week-long experience being non-resistant to the resistance which he experiences from others. I would like you not to separate yourself from Jesus in the account of the story because you know that our lives are filled with resistance. The resistance comes from personalities; it comes through mates; it comes through financial problems; through death of loved ones. They come out of the blue: from people taking advantage of us, stealing money from us, or putting us in places where we didn't want to be. The resistances appear like the old cash registers when you pushed the button down, the price pops-up in front of you. Well, it seems like we didn't even push the button and the resistance appeared before us. We all have a great vision for our lives, and moving through the natural and usual resistances is the major issue to our being able to fulfill that life desire, which usually is more life, a more fulfilled life, and a more expressive life.

Jesus stated clearly, "I came that you might have life and that you might have it more abundantly." And he didn't teach that only through words, he taught it through the living activity of his life. One of those activities is seen in the example of the last week of his life. Judas did not want Jesus to enter Jerusalem on a mule; he wanted him to come on a white horse with an army behind him. It was that letdown of Judas' vision for Jesus that caused Judas to sell him out. But, as Jesus rode

Chapter 10: The Path of Non-Resistance

into town, Judas wasn't his only resistance. There were the Pharisees whom he began to hear mumbling, sneaking, and talking about setting-up Jesus and turning him in to the Romans. The resistance comes to Jesus through Judas, obviously, who sells him for thirty pieces of silver. Much of Christian interpretation of Judas has been critical of Judas, calling Judas bad and telling us to not like Judas. Unity's gift in the Easter week scene is how they have interpreted Judas: Judas is essential—without Judas one loses the risk of losing one's life, of dying to one's self—for the potential of resurrection. Look at those resistances in your life: the ones you want to eliminate and the ones you find discomforting, and give them some consideration in this lesson as issues which are provided by God as a means for transforming you into the object and goal of your life. You don't have to turn them into 'good'; you don't have to make them out to be not 'bad'; they are means for accomplishing God's purpose through you, whether you see it at this point in time or not.

So is the role of Peter like that of Judas. What has the Christian church done with Peter who denied Jesus three times? They have 'whipped' him, telling us not to be like Peter. Yet, Peter is a very important part of Jesus' inner testing and Jesus' having to continually come to terms with himself. Even Jesus needed to recognize: if you want to make it through the inner testing, ultimately you must make the decision to do it with yourself, unto yourself and within yourself. You must draw upon your own resources, authority, leadership, brilliance, and genius. And the capacity to follow through with courage requires being able to draw the wisdom, the skills, and the resources from within. I may have a partner, I may have a support group, but they are only there to mirror to me that it is here within me—draw it from within—God lives within me, the Christ lives within me and from that I draw the sustaining power. When it comes down to the ultimate moments in life[64], the friends walk out. After you have lost somebody very special, your friends have to leave; they have to go on with their lives, and then you are alone with yourself. When you begin a great business venture everybody may come to the cracking of the champagne, but then on Monday morning you are there all alone. When I came here in 1970, I can remember my mother calling me after I had given my first lesson. It had been a wonderful morning—60 people had shown up, and the

---

[64] Where God is asking you to expand, to define your inner knowing, and engage with non-resistance. (Ed.)

Chapter 10: The Path of Non-Resistance

Sunday before there had only been 20—I was all excited. My mother asked me the simple question, "What are you going to do Monday morning?" I don't know! I'll be all alone—all those folks who were so devoted to Unity are going to have to go to work and here I am.

Another resistance that comes to Jesus takes place in the Garden of Gethsemane—a wonderful scene. He goes in with his disciples and says, "Why don't you stay here—I need to go and pray for awhile." He goes into the Garden of Gethsemane and leans on a rock and, there he prays, "Father, if it is possible, would you please take this cup from me." Do you ever feel like that? That is the path of least resistance: if I can get out of this, please find me a way; let me take the easy road—and the easy road is always backwards. The easy road does not allow you to stay right where you are so you can watch and step into where you are about to become. We always want to run back—that is human nature. Palm Sunday and Easter week deals with stepping into life—the taking-on of life's issues—rather than running out of the Garden. And remember, there is nothing wrong with running out of the Garden. A lot of the human race does—running-out is human nature. Stepping-in is exploring the creative, the Divine. After Jesus asks the question, he steps out of the garden and returns to his friends who are sleeping and says, "Aren't you even going to stay awake with me?" He has to give up on them. Once again he is being tossed into his own self. He returns to the garden and says, "Okay God, if you can't take the cup then I'll consider drinking it," meaning, "I will go to the cross." And once again, he has to drop the issue and move out of the Garden. And when he goes back in he says, "I am full of sorrow and terror." So are we all. You step into the unknown and you ought to feel sorrow and dread. Those are scary moments. Then finally he says, "Okay, I'll drink the cup." He walks out and says, "I must fulfill the Scriptures." Then the next resistance is Pilate. And we know what he does with Pilate. He says to Pilate, "If the truth is what you say it is, I will not resist or move on with my life."

What is the issue on Palm Sunday? The issue is that if we can cooperate with the occurrences and resistances in our life, then we have an opportunity for genius. If you can find a way not to oppose those situations that put up walls and barriers of resistance and frustration, there is another possibility for your life and for all lives involved. Naturally, you find that you want to resist and fight: fight the pain, fight the struggle, fight the personality, and fight what looks to be

Chapter 10: The Path of Non-Resistance

ahead, or fight what is the next opportunity. And, if you can find a way to cooperate with all that, then there is an opportunity to relax, which allows you to find a way through and beyond. That is the transformative experience—you step into newness, openness, and rocky insecurity, until the formation of clarity and the new being takes place. And that can happen every second of the day if you are willing to practice non-resistance.

There is the image of a man who imagines himself as a prisoner in a cell. He stands at one end of a small, dark barren room on his toes with arms outstretched upward. Hands grasp for support onto a small barred window, the room's only apparent source of light. If he holds on tight, straining toward the window, turning his head just so, he can see just a bit of bright sunlight, barely visible between the uppermost bars. This light is his only hope. He will not risk losing it. [As you read this, think how much we hold on to the hope or on to the present light that we see, thinking that is all there is.] So, he continues to strain towards that bit of light, holding tightly to the bars. So committed are his efforts not to lose sight of the glimmer of life-giving light, that it never occurs to him to let go, explore the darkness of the rest of the cell, so it is that he never discovers the door at the end of the cell is

The Path of God

open and that he is free—he has always been free to walk out into the day, if only he would let go. Even holding on to the light can be a limit—entering into the darkness is a way to work with transformation via resistance.

So, one option is to cooperate with the resistance and to not resist what is occurring. Another way is to hold on to what is and to resist the resistance, and even then you are not wrong. A possibility is to not resist your need to be resistant. You see, some people will read this message and say within, "I have to not resist anything." So, they go home only to experience increased resistance. The point is not to stop being resistant, it is a deeper inner message—don't even resist the inner resistance.

It is also possible with this system of teaching to do both. So, you can be non-resistant, you can be resistant and non-resistant to being resistant, and you can also find yourself like Jesus in the Garden of Gethsemane. What does he do? He walks-in and he works with himself. The whole issue is to work within—process yourself. Maybe you need to go for counseling to help with the processing; maybe you need to go to a weekend seminar or talk to a good friend; but help process yourself out. Just don't ignore it. Jesus walks into the Garden and says, "This is just too much for me, I am not going to resist my inner resistance to this." So, he walks out, takes a breath of air, walks back in and says, "I am getting closer, closer to cooperating, but I am not still sure I can do what's asked." So, he walks out again, not resisting his resistance to the demand. Then he gets greater strength and says, "Ah, now I can walk through." Another option: So, you can be non-resistant; you can be resistant and not resistant to the resistance; and you can play them both out, and that is probably the way life goes—move a step forward, then take one back. You know how we judge ourselves, because we move forward and then take a step backwards—my God, that is the process. Life is a dance—it isn't a thrust—it is a step forward then back, and then gracefully, we hope; we move forward again.

Definitions of Non-Resistance, Resistance, and Least Resistance

I have some information that I developed which explains non-resistance, resistance, and the path of least resistance.

Non-Resistance

When encountering an external or internal resistance, block, or change—which is uncomfortable to your present direction or habit—rather than responding with the usual habitual response, you relax, let go of your position, your habits, and agree to cooperate with the movement whether the resistance is from the outside or from within the personality or ego, etc. Here is an example: Your husband or wife comes home and says, "We're moving to Oshkosh, Wisconsin."

And immediately, all of the resistances go up inside: "We can't go. I don't know anybody there. What will the kids do in school?" Maybe you have a kid with whom you live who is a pain in the neck—they come home with a 'punk' hairdo, colored orange, looking like a creature out of Mars. Immediately, the resistances go up, the resistances say, "I don't want my kid to look like this… they're not going to live in this house if they look like that." In that situation, you would relax your usual habitual response, which is, "No, I can't do this, I won't do this, I won't participate." When you relax, you step out of the habit, you take a breath, and you agree to cooperate. That does not mean that you give license or that you say it is right—it just says that some part of you agrees to cooperate with what is. That is just the first step. You take the first step and then after you have taken it you may again

Chapter 10: The Path of Non-Resistance

say, "Oh, my God, I can't do this, this is impossible, I can't stand this pain inside me." Your mate has just told you they are having an affair—your first reaction is to KILL—it's the right reaction! You have made a commitment to test out a whole new system of activity. So, your usual response is ready to 'slug' him/her and as you go to push your fist through, something inside says, "Let's try non-resistance." You think you can't do that, but you remember the principle. You relax, take a step back and get open to cooperate. You don't know at this time what 'cooperate' means, but you have taken the inner position. Is that clear? It doesn't mean anything about what you may do. You may still kill him! You may still throw the kid out, but you take that inner pose.

Look at what Jesus does with Judas. Judas says, "I'm the one who sold you out." Sure, from the record it shows that Jesus was angry. He was sorrowful and he was full of dread and fear. I am sure he must have been one tense man: don't you think? I would be. I wouldn't be very non-resistant to that trip—it is a very painful death, crucifixion. Can you imagine when Judas says, "I am the one," what Jesus' normal, usual reaction would be? And it is a right reaction. It is a right, natural reaction to want to clobber, resist, or kill the resistance—but we are seeking to move the race on, aren't we? It raises the question, if the commitment is made—what is the principle? What am I committed to? Non-resistance? So Jesus must have breathed in and said, "Okay... I agree to cooperate." He doesn't know how that will evidence within or what will be required. But in that action, the being definitely moves on. I cannot give you a long, drawn out process of the catharsis— of what will happen—I can suggest just take the pose; the inner pose is what is important.

Let's say you desire to give up cigarettes, liquor, an attitude, maybe an obsession, or an attraction. Something inside you really desires to do it and immediately you hear the resistance that rises up saying, "God, I can't do that, what would I be like without the alcohol? ...I might look like I don't know how to live—I can't." Take a breath, step away, step back, and listen to the inner desire and say within, "I agree to cooperate with the inner desire." Now, whether you can last just one second cooperating—that is still a step in behalf of the race consciousness and yourself.

Chapter 10: The Path of Non-Resistance

Living in Non-Resistance

Now, why would you take on a commitment to non-resistance? Does it sound stupid? On what philosophical base are we building such a pose? There are three important fundamental Universal Principles upon which you either structure your life or you don't. If you can 'buy' these Principles, then you can live the law of non-resistance. If you cannot, you will have to live the law of resistance or the law of least resistance.

Nothing to Fear including Fear

The first is: there is nothing to fear in the Universe including fear. Knowing this and trying it out, you can do it. You say, "Okay, Judas, I agree to cooperate." And the only reason you can say it is you understand there is nothing to fear in Judas, including my own fears of him. To follow this further, then I don't fear the pain of my sorrow. For example: some people, when they start doing the work of the Prayer of the Heart, say it hurts to bring the attention into the heart. Immediately, they want to leave it. Well, of course our hearts will hurt when we bring attention to them. Our hearts have been abandoned. We haven't had contact with our heart—so when we go inside we begin to feel the pain. The only answer I can offer: don't resist the pain. Go through the pain. If you have never cried for your mother, one day you must cry because you lost your mother. If you have never cried because you lost a mate who walked out on you and 'ruined' your life, someday you are going to have to go through the pain of that. You can block it and resist it for just so long—that is what resistance is—until one day you will be brought up against it. You are going to have to cry the tears. The body knows what it is intended to do and so does the emotional system. There is nothing to fear in the Universe including fear. Don't resist the fear, friends. Don't knock it out with an affirmation or a treasure map.

Trust the Activity and the Players

The second principle, you can trust all activities and players in the game. Do you believe that? Do you believe you can trust your kids to play out their 'punkness'? Well, they are going to. They will either do it in front of you or behind your back. I had a funny experience the other day. I'm taking a computer course and I went in to pick up my papers and they were all checked 'minus'. I haven't had a minus check in years. I was real angry at the teacher. I'm not going back to the class! Somehow, that has to do with this issue—I don't trust the players in the game.

God's Intention is Expansion and Creativity

The third principle: God's intention is expansion and creativity. Do you believe that? Do you believe that the loss of your daughter is part of her expansion and creativity? Do you believe you lost your husband because a part of the Universe's intention is your expansion and creativity and his? Do you or don't you? You better come to terms with it. Do you believe you lost your business because God's intention is expansion and creativity? Jesus, do you believe you lost your life because God's intention is expansion and creativity? Do you? Wake up—make a commitment folks. The most important thing in life is your commitment to what you believe and then to live your life accordingly. If you sit on the fence, you will never know what to stand behind.

Living in Resistance

Now let's talk about the issue of resistance—what would living in resistance be like? When encountering an external or internal resistance, block, change, which is uncomfortable to your present direction or habit, you respond with your initial response or usual habit. And you are either fully conscious of doing that or on the brink of seeing that. In the example of a new situation coming into your life, or a new career or a new personality or a suggestion of change, you resist by whining, grumbling, complaining, gossiping, or proving your point. You generally spend 'years' saying why it can't work or won't work or shouldn't work and then you dig up all the reasons why it shouldn't—it is 'terrific research'. You spend hours doing it. If you are Jesus living in this principle of resistance, you would go to the disciples and say, "Judas is trying to hurt me. Now, I want you to help me out because Judas is bad." And then you gossip. You spend lots of time gossiping and figuring out a plan of how to take care of Judas and all the reasons why he is wrong and why his way just won't work. If you are in the Garden of Gethsemane you tell God he is no good and you leave. And then you get all your friends to agree that God isn't good. If you desire to give up cigarettes, liquor or some attitude, you believe, "Oh, well, I can't live without cigarettes anyway, etc. It is too good to be true."

Why do we respond like that? I think the point is clear. We believe at our base root that there is something to fear in the Universe—"somebody can damage me." Folks, if you want to live like

Chapter 10: The Path of Non-Resistance

that, go ahead—just honor that you live the life of resistance and do it well! Do it with dignity and pride. Build your own church based upon resistance. You should attract a huge crowd! Next, you believe that the Universe wants to stay exactly as it is. And you are going to have a hard time—it will be like holding the ocean back. And you can believe that the Universe is devoted to a closed system—you know it all, and you want to control it and manipulate it.[65]

Living in Least Resistance

What is the path of least resistance? When encountering an external or internal resistance, block or change which is uncomfortable to your present direction or habit, you continue to do what you have always done—even though something deeply urges you from a point of ongoing discomfort to move in the direction of action on your behalf. That is the path of least resistance. This is the way the Universe 'rolls down'. You wake in the morning and say, "Gosh, I really should go on a diet." And incidentally, I

---

[65] When living in resistance the typical thought is to believe you are "making it right" and it is difficult to see that it actually is manipulation. (Ed.)

am not interested in whether weight or non-weight is good or bad—I don't frankly know the difference. But you wake in the morning and say, "Boy, I ought to really take off some weight." And you lie there and say, "Oh, but this is easier," that's all—that is the path of least resistance. You hear inside yourself, "You know, I really ought to call so-and-so and take on this issue—they really owe me money." And then your mind goes, "Oh, my God, I may end up in court—it's just easier to forget the whole thing." And so you put on 'weight' in the head and 'weight' in the body or 'weight' in the emotions.

The Practice of Non-Resistance

Now, if any of this is reaching you—how does one practice non-resistance?

Face Adversity

First, put yourself in the face of adversity. You must. In the story of Jacob from the Book of Genesis, Jacob takes on the angel and wrestles with it. You have to wrestle with yourself if you want to move forward. The beautiful result about Jacob's wrestling with the angel is that he looks at the angel at one point and says, "Not until you call me blessed will I let you go." "Not until this

Chapter 10: The Path of Non-Resistance

event blesses me will I let it go." And the blessing is becoming open to move forward.

I watched it happen this week. Two weeks ago a member of our staff was working with an issue in publications. She was wondering how we could get over 1,000 booklets bound for sales. She felt totally stuck. Her comments were, "There aren't enough people around to help; we don't have the money to pay for staffing; we don't have a large enough binder. What are we going to do about it?" Then I saw her sit back quietly while everybody else talked and I knew something tremendous was going on inside. All of a sudden, from out of nowhere, BANG she stood up, threw her coffee in excitement and said, "I've got it!" She had wrestled with her angel—deeply, internally. Many years ago, I bumped into terror with regard to stepping out onto a concert stage as a concert pianist. You know what I had to do? I had to step out onto a concert stage and wrestle with myself there.

I have never told this on a Sunday morning, but when I was twelve years old I stole a watch at Grover Cronin's in Waltham, Massachusetts. It was about a twenty or thirty dollar watch which was a lot in those days, and I remember the horror when my mother found out I had stolen it so I could give it to her for Mother's Day. She looked at me and she said, "Carol, we're going to have to take that back and give it to the manager."

> *Friend, hope for the Guest while you are alive. Jump into experience while you are alive! Think... and think... while you are alive. What you call 'salvation' belongs to the time before death.*
>
> *If you don't break your ropes while you're alive, do you think ghosts will do it after?*
>
> *The idea that the soul will join with the ecstatic just because it is rotten—that is all fantasy. What is found now is found then. If you find nothing new, you will simply end up with an apartment in the City of Death. If you make love with the divine now, in the next life you will have the face of satisfied desire.*
>
> *So plunge into the truth, find out who the Teacher is, believe in the Great Sound!*
>
> *Kabir says this: When the Guest is being searched for, it is the intensity of the longing for the Guest that does all the work. Look at me, and you will see a slave of that intensity.*[66]

---

[66] *The Kabir Book*, p. 24

Chapter 10: The Path of Non-Resistance

Listen to your Internal Being

Second, you must listen. I watched another member of our staff working with a situation. She came into a meeting this week and as she sat there, I was telling her about an area where she might expand in terms of her personal ministry. Somebody else was sitting with us, and we shared an idea of how she might see herself becoming. The first thing I saw come up was the resistance. We kept sharing and then I watched the person go way inside and listen. She began to listen not only to her inner self but to the outer selves (those of us giving feedback). She really listened. And when she listened, she heard, and after about fifteen minutes of deep work, she said, "Thank you, I really see it and I am going to act on it." She listened.

Jacob listened when he wrestled with the angel. That first woman whom I talked about, who finally came up with an idea of how to work with this, listened. I listened to my inner being when I was twelve years old; I listened to my mother and I listened to the manager. He counseled me about the danger I was in. Jesus listened to a deep part of himself when he was in the Garden of Gethsemane, and he didn't listen only to himself when his self was saying 'no', he listened deeper.

> *The flute of interior time is played whether we hear it or not. What we mean by 'love' is its sound coming in.*
>
> *When love hits the farthest edge of excess, it reaches a wisdom, and the fragrance of that knowledge! It penetrates our thick bodies, it goes through walls—Its network of notes has a structure as if a million suns were arranged inside.*
>
> *This tune has truth in it. Where else have you heard a sound like this?* [67]

Move into Creativity

Finally, participating in non-resistance moves one into creativity. Jacob, by wrestling with the angel and listening, becomes the leader of Israel. The woman, who experienced the difficulty with the issue of binding booklets, went inside and listened, exploded into creativity. She ended up 'creating' you folks to help her with the project and in one week, finished binding 1,000 booklets that she hadn't been able to touch for eight months. I talked about the terror on the concert stage. How did I finally handle that? I left performing on the concert stage. You can walk away. You don't have to stay. Groping with the

---

[67] *The Kabir Book*, p. 21

Chapter 10: The Path of Non-Resistance

issue, becoming non-resistant to it, doesn't mean you have to stay—you can leave, if it comes from the profundity of your inner listening rather than your escape mechanism. Go beneath it. Go deeply into the deeper message. In terms of my stealing the watch, I listened and I discovered that I had to honor my guilt, and it taught me that I cannot do that again. And in terms of Jesus—his genius was revealed when he broke through a cross, and he was resurrected.

> *My inside, listen to me, the greatest spirit, the Teacher is near, wake up, wake up!*
>
> *Run to his feet—he is standing close to your head right now.*
>
> *You have slept for millions and millions of years.*
>
> *Why not wake up this morning?* [68]

---

[68] *The Kabir Book*, P.17

The Path of God

*8: Carol Ruth Knox sharing and honoring her Inner Voice
(She is explaining 'The Prayer of the Heart'. Some words on
the podium are deliberately blurred)*

11: THE PATH OF DEATH & RESURRECTION

March 30, 1986

Symbols for Easter

In this Easter lesson, my intention is to share with you a great Principle which we often ignore: the Principle of Life. When we think about life, we often consider that life is the opposite of death—but it isn't. Life is larger than death and is larger than birth. (A non-dual life includes birth and death, life and death). Life incorporates both birth and death; it stands as a fundamental, holding both within itself as the larger Principle that transcends both birth and dying. If a person can step into that Principle, remembering that Life is always working on their behalf, then their personal life can be expanded and transformed. It is that Life Principle that we salute, that we celebrate on Easter, and that we really must celebrate throughout our lifetimes. When we move out of duality into non-duality, we understand that non-duality incorporates the Principle of Life and Life holds precious both birth and death. And it is a Principle of our life that lives richly in our hearts and our souls and in that transparent part of ourselves that is larger than the body itself. When we step into that, then life doesn't become a burden, it doesn't become an effort, it doesn't become something we work at—it becomes something that we live, and it lives us as we step into it. I know that Jesus knew this well. That is the Principle he entered when he entered the tomb on that Good Friday night and prepared himself for what we have called Easter (which is really a springtime celebration that we connect with the resurrection of Jesus of Nazareth).

The Walnut

When we hold a walnut, we see living within its seed, a mighty Principle, the Principle of Life. When we touch that life (which can't be seen, can't be held) and when we realize its innermost sense, we recognize that we do not have to do anything to prove that life within the seed. This walnut shell does not have to do anything within itself to prove that life is within it; it does not have to teach life to itself; it does not have to affirm it. Some of us have walked-around and thought that in our religious life or in our spiritual life, we had to affirm something, we had to do something

Chapter 11: The Path of Death & Resurrection

about it, we had to create something, or we had to empower something. Well, don't you see that life itself does not have to do anything about itself or to itself? You don't have to prod it; you don't have to teach it; you don't have to affirm it; you don't have to coach it; you don't have to beg it; you don't have to cajole it—your life lives you. Your life is bigger than your birth. Your life is bigger than your death. Your life is an 'is-ness' that moves you, that creates you, that builds you, that shoves you, that pushes you, and that expands you.

This walnut knows that and lives it. We tend to spend so much time trying to get to something which already is—trying to get to something—the secret of Easter is to simply be what Life is within you and let it process you. Let it grow you. The life inside this walnut works in spite of externals. We see that same reality when we see a piece of grass break through concrete that life force in the grass lives in spite of the external. You must know that. You must come to know that, and your life will become a different kind of experience. It will be an experience of elegant joy that is deeper than joy versus sorrow. It will become the happening of love that is bigger than love versus hate, something we do not yet have words to describe in our English language. You see the Principle that is working inside of this nut works deeper than birth or death. It cracks the present world, whether it is a seed cover or an egg shell or an umbilical cord. That Life does the cracking.

The Egg

Let me use the same analogy with an egg. The reason we use eggs at Easter is because we know that something wonderful takes place inside an egg, and we can show it to our children. We love to have our children observe the egg and understand the process of chickens breaking through eggs into life. What we are appreciating even more deeply in such a moment in the 'something' that is going on inside of this egg. There is a Principle. You can't see it. You can't taste it. You can't touch it. But the Principle works the egg. That Principle will grow inside of the egg, and gradually when the time comes (because all of us are inside tombs/wombs) this shell will crack. Most of us are frightened at the shell cracking. But the Principle of Life is working, and it must crack shells; it must take off seed covers; it must thrust babies through wombs; it must force 'Jesuses' out of tombs. It must.

Take a moment to go inside yourself. Don't shut your eyes, but try to make contact with this

Chapter 11: The Path of Death & Resurrection

Principle in you. This is what Easter is about. Easter is not about only going out for brunch; it is not only about beautiful clothes; it is not only about money. Easter is more deeply about your tapping inside you and realizing how casually we all hold our life. How casually, without thought, we never consider what brought us into existence. (You cannot take a life, life is. There is no birth and no death). Do you ever consider the priceless thing that happened to you the day you were conceived? We have issues about abortion and about what is right and what is wrong regarding taking life, but you can't take life—you can't kill life. Life is. Life knows itself. Yet, we ignore its wonder. We forget that at some precious moment in time, our life was transported into a seed. That seed was a tomb. And the larger vehicle we were inside was a womb. And incorporated into all of that was this Principle, Life. But just because something was placed into a womb; just because something came into some new kind of form does not mean that it didn't exist before and that it won't exist after. This is Life we are talking about—it is a stream and as it progresses: it rolls into form; it takes on form to work the form; and then it cracks the form and pushes out the limits of those forms. It must.

The Path of God

It continues to crack and move into larger shapes of life, until at some point in time we say, "It dies." But it was never really born and it never really dies—it is just Life living itself—and it is indomitable. It is in you, it gave birth to you, it formed you, it loved you, and it grew you without your having to do a thing about it—no action, no thought, no desire on your part, no plan or design, but something precious expands itself and that is called Life. That is the reason Jesus said, "I came so that you might have Life and that you might have it more abundantly." He was not talking about life with regard to birth. He was saying, "I came that I might put you in touch with the fact that there is an indomitable power in you, and you can trust it. No matter what happens to your life; no matter how tough it gets; no matter how much lack; no matter how badly you have been treated; no matter how brutally you have been beaten; this Life that I have come to give you more abundantly is a power that exceeds even your life experience. It far exceeds your birth or death. Make contact with it. Make a commitment to it. Sing about it. Get up and shout about it! And when you do, you will inspire others: to see that you know; to allow them to tap into it; to touch it, so that their life might have the bountifulness that you emanate through your eyes, through the living of your life, that says—you know and you trust Life."

The Tomb in Easter

Consider this poem. It will serve as a bridge to something else that occurs in Easter. Yes, Easter is a celebration of life. But Easter is also about a tomb: that walnut is about a seed breaking, an egg is about a shell cracking, a child's being born is about a womb being opened, and Easter is about some man putting himself in a tomb which then cracks wide open. Easter is not only Life living itself; Easter is also the activity in death taking place in a tomb.

> *Whoever you are: some evening take a step out of your house, which you know so well.* [69]

Take a step out of your house which you know so well. That is what Jesus did. He put himself on a cross and then threw himself into a tomb and that activity was taking a step out of his house that he knew so well. The greatest difficulty about being reborn in the midst of life is that too many of us

---

[69] Rainer Maria Rilke (Ed.)

want to keep our present house; we never want to step outside the known.

> *Whoever you are: some evening take a step out of your house, which you know so well.*
>
> *Enormous space is near, your house lies where it begins, whoever you are.*
>
> *Your eyes find it hard to tear themselves from the sloping threshold, but with your eyes slowly, slowly, lift one black tree up, so it stands against the sky, skinny, alone.*
>
> *With that you have made the world. The world is immense and like a word that is still growing in the silence.*
>
> *In the same moment that your will grasps it, your eyes, feeling its subtlety, will leave it.*[70]

Easter also involves a tomb. Here is a statement from Hermann Hesse's, *Demian-The Story of Emil Sinclair's Youth*:

> *The bird fights its way out of the egg. The egg is the world. Who would be born must first destroy a world. The bird flies to God.*

---

[70] *Selected Poems of Rainer Maria Rilke*, p. 71

Chapter 11: The Path of Death & Resurrection

In our tradition, we are not comfortable in 'breaking the world'. Life involves death and rebirth continuously, and you and I must participate. If we don't, we stagnate. We must continually be put in dark tombs/wombs so that we can be born again. And if we try to stay in ease, if we try to keep 'it' easy, then we feel stagnation, dissipation, boredom begin to settle in. And you can apply this to any area of your life: the relationships that you try to keep comfortable or your sense of yourself that you try to keep comfortable. The symbolism of Easter is that Jesus stepped out of ease. He had it 'made'… you know. He stepped out of ease. You too must. And you know if you don't participate, you stagnate, you dry up, and you can feel it. We know we have entered into the tomb when we feel the subtle signals of discomfort. Sometimes it will be a band of tightness around the head that won't go away—that is a 'tomb feeling'. It will be a flutter of fear that occurs in the belly, and for some reason, you just can't get rid of the fear this time—it walks around with you. All the affirming and all the special courses, aiming to break free of the discomfort, don't work. It just stays with you. You have been pushed into the tomb. You have been pushed out of ease. Life is forcing you—that Life is bigger than birth and death and is forcing you to some deeper space. You know you are in the tomb when you start feeling annoyed with yourself. Do you ever feel that?

You know, life really doesn't begin until you are forty! I used to hear that line, and I wondered how it could be true. Why is that so? Because you don't really get nervous about life until you are forty. You don't really feel it begin to close down until then. You don't ever really have the thought, "You know, maybe I'm going to lose it," until you are around forty. And that feeling of beginning to lose it is a really powerful thing. It is the signal that says you may think you have a line on living (and you do—you can trust life), but if you want to participate and struggle through the gradual pull of death that is going on around you—the death of personality, the death of thinking you have got it made, or the death of your career—if you want to keep breaking through, there is a struggle involved. You must participate. Jesus did.

Sometimes the way the tomb shows is an immobilizing career position or a sense that everything is slowing down or some recognition that you haven't grown in the past ten years and you are beginning to look for a good crisis: "I'm still the same old soul I was ten years ago. I must grow to keep feeling life." That is a tomb. Sometimes it is a call for freedom that is unable to

Chapter 11: The Path of Death & Resurrection

be denied. You know you can be freer than you are. You walk into situations and you say, "I could be more than this." or "When am I going to get rid of these parts of my personality."

Here is a quotation from a work by Opitz in *The Freeman* journal.

> *It is obvious that a creature of such vast potential as man is not designed to float with the current; he is designed to go against the stream and he enhances his powers by so doing. We didn't volunteer for this business of living; we were—you might say—drafted into life, and for life. We're here, to learn, and to grow. The moment we rest on our oars and begin to think we've got it made, at that moment we start to come unglued. Biologically speaking, we are embarked upon a lost cause. But when we truly participate in life, we discover other dimensions than the merely biological. Life becomes a cosmic adventure, an adventure in destiny; a new kind and quality of life begins to evolve in us, and we come face to face with the eternal mysteries.*[71]

That is what Jesus was doing in that tomb/womb/seed cover/shell that day—coming to terms with the eternal mystery.

And here is another statement from Rilke:

---

[71] Edmond A. Opitz, *The Freeman*, August, 1963

> *It's possible I am pushing through solid rock in flintlike layers, as the ore lies alone; I am such a long way in I see no way through, and no space: everything is close to my face, and everything close to my face is stone.*
>
> *I don't have much knowledge yet in grief—so this massive darkness makes me small.*
>
> *You be the master: make yourself fierce, break in: then your great transforming will happen to me, and my great grief cry will happen to you.*[72]

Feel it. Here is the place where you must go against the stream. Here you must enhance your powers or the tomb/womb will capture you and we all know that. So, the walnut must move toward the light; the egg must crack through the shell; the child must protrude through the womb to be born; Jesus must shatter the prison walls. It says in Philippians 3:14, "I press towards the mark for the prize is the high calling of God... " And what is the prize? The prize is cracking the shell—a rich feeling. The prize is cutting the umbilical cord—a rich feeling. The prize is moving the stone from the tomb—a rich feeling.

---

[72] *Selected Poems of Rainer Maria Rilke*, #19, p. 55

Chapter 11: The Path of Death & Resurrection

What Occurs In the Tomb?

This brings us to what is going on in the tomb. What is going on in the tomb? Well, Life certainly; Life that is larger than birth and death. Certainly Life is going on in the tomb—you can trust that one. You don't have to do a thing about Life. Life is bigger than birth and death. Life is what is living in the walnut, cracking it out. Life is what is living in the interior of the egg, cracking the shell. Life is what is living a baby, pushing it through the womb. Life doesn't struggle to survive—it just does. But we must participate with death so that we can move into birth into death into birth. Neither is greater than the other. But we must participate with birth and death. So, Life certainly goes on.

And as it certainly goes on, we realize that something else, very special is happening inside the tomb. Certainly, metaphorically, one must take off one's clothes. It says that when they went to the tomb that morning that Jesus' clothes were lying on the ground outside the tomb. Can you imagine what Jesus felt like when he changed his body in that tomb and found that the clothes he had on no longer fit, and he could carry them out with nobility and lay them on the ground and say, "Here, God, I give them to you, I don't need them any more." So, certainly inside the tomb, Life was not only living, but also Jesus was participating—he took off his clothes: the walnut must take off its seed cover; the egg must split its shell; the child must cut the umbilical cord; you will have to drop your personality or weaknesses or whatever you know is finished. You will have to let go of holding onto the 'easy'. You will have to give up the liquor or the food or the cigarettes or the thing that is holding you back, and you know it is not 'should' forcing you into this tomb—Life pushed you in. You must take off your clothes and leave them on the ground with pride saying, "There, I give these to you, look at me—I am a new person." You must take off your clothes.

And once you take off those clothes, then certainly there must also be silence. Oh, friends, how we avoid silence. And even this service is a kind of 'lie' against silence, because the deeper spiritual work is done in silence. And we Westerners hate that word. We don't want to foster it or nourish it. But can you imagine what Jesus was doing in the silence of that tomb? What goes on in that silence? Well, you wait a long time. And what do you wait for? Well, if you are that piece of grass growing through concrete, you are waiting to see the empty spaces that will appear:

Chapter 11: The Path of Death & Resurrection

that will be the message that says, "The light is coming in, you may now grow through the cracks." That is what you do in the silence. You wait. You wait for the empty spaces to appear in the grey concrete that says, "This is where you go next;" and that calls for listening, subtle listening for the next idea, the next way, the next amount of information, the next light, and the next body form.

There is no greater drama than Easter. And the drama has to do with 'cracking the shell'—as Jesus trusted Life, as he participated in taking the clothes off, and as he stood in the silence. In that silence some great signal must have stepped through that tomb moving him beyond the walls of his present limits. It says in Luke 24 that Jesus was walking along the road to Emmaus, "and they didn't even recognize him." Sometimes wouldn't you like it if 'they' didn't even recognize you because you had become such a new person? Our traditional friends would call that a 'new person in Christ'… it really is a 'new person in Life'. That occurs because you have given up your limits so that you might become so new that they might not even recognize you; and what they won't recognize is not your body, but a sense about you; that you have grasped onto something phenomenal and it leads your life and it lives your life and it empowers your life; and you are bigger than birth and death because you know Life. It says that when Jesus appeared another time before Thomas and the other Disciples, they didn't even see him enter the room because he could move into the emptiness between the spaces in the material world of personality or physicality or relationship—you can move so clearly that even walls don't get in your way. What a marvelous Principle! He stepped through the walls and they had to place their hands into the holes[73] to even see if this was the same person.

Closing

Easter is about Life. Life that is richer and bigger than birth and death. You can die knowing you are Life. You can die knowing you are Life and that Life works in your behalf. Live your life accordingly. Carry it with you. Cry it out! And to get there, you have to crack shells, you have to go into tombs, and if you resist, you will stagnate. And although Life cannot be killed, if you resist, you will know somewhere along the way that you

---

[73] Metaphorical reference to St. Thomas and his need to touch the wounds (holes) of Jesus to recognize and acknowledge his emergence from death. (Ed.)

Chapter 11: The Path of Death & Resurrection

lost your chance; and although you cannot be lost because you cannot be anything but saved, you can lose your chance to grow, to crack the shell, and to cut through the grey limited walls of consciousness.

In closing:

> *I find you in all these things of the world that I love calmly, like a brother; in things no one cares for you brood like a seed; and to powerful things you give an immense power.*
>
> *Strength plays such a marvelous game—it moves through the things of the world like a servant, groping out in roots, tapering in trunks, and in the treetops like a rising from the dead.* [74]

---

[74] *Selected Poems of Rainer Maria Rilke*, #11, p. 33

9: Carol Ruth Knox speaking at Unity of Walnut Creek (Coy and Carol Martha Cross are in the background [right]. Some faces have been deliberately blurred.)

ENGAGE WITH COY F. CROSS II

Coy Cross II on Facebook

https://www.facebook.com/CoyFCrossIIPhd

Coy Cross II on YouTube

http://www.youtube.com/channel/UCfb8JPMD9P46pQHLmE1uN0Q

Coy Cross on the Web

Search "Coy F Cross" for interviews and more.

Coy Cross II on Twitter

https://twitter.com/coy_ii

Carol Ruth Knox and Coy F. Cross II

For more information about Carol Ruth Knox and her pioneering spiritual work visit:

http://CarolRuthKnox.com

https://www.facebook.com/RevCarolRuthKnoxPhd

Transformational Workshops with Coy Cross II

> Being Fully Present in Caregiving
>
> Dealing with Crisis in Caregiving
>
> Practical Spirituality

Email: transformation@thedhance.com

Coy Cross II in Print

> ***The Dhance: A Caregiver's Search for Meaning* by Coy F. Cross II, Ph.D.**
>
> Practical Spiritual Help for a Crisis

Buy it now!   http://TheDhance.com

Coy F. Cross II PhD

A Message from Coy F. Cross II, Author, about <u>*The Dhance*</u>

In 2009, life presented me with the opportunity to know God on a more personal level. My precious wife Carol Martha and I were told she had Stage 3, Level C ovarian cancer. This wasn't the path I'd expect on my way to God, but this is the path I've been given. These past three years [2009-2012] have been my 'graduate course' in deepening my relationship with the Divine. I have experienced a curious mixture of great pain and great joy. I have seen God in the faces of doctors, nurses, cancer patients and grieving families. There has been an abundance of loving kindness from perfect strangers. Finally, I have loved and been loved more deeply than I could ever imagine. I have come to know that God is right here, right now, in the midst of this terrible disease called cancer. But my search isn't over and I don't expect it to reach its end until my end. "Wherever I am, God is, and all is well."

Testimonials

> *This book is a story of life at its best in the worst of experiences in the human journey. It gives us hope that we can always grow and discover who we truly are and what is important in life. A love story filled with life skills.* —Rev. Beth Ann Suggs, PCC; Unity Minister

More than a powerful love story, <u>The Dhance</u> serves as a Spiritual Practice guide to courageously working through a major life crisis. —Greg Finch, Licensed Teacher, Unity Worldwide Ministries

Unity of Walnut Creek

http://www.unityofwalnutcreek.com/

A supportive spiritual community

Prayer support

Spiritual growth

Classes and workshops

Making a difference

A Detailed History of Carol Ruth Knox at Unity of Walnut Creek

http://data.unityofwalnutcreek.com/information/history_of_unity_01.pdf

Unity of Walnut Creek Historical Timeline

http://www.unityofwalnutcreek.com/walnut-creek-timeline

KOHO PONO LLC

https://kohopono.com/

Read Our Authors

    Coy F. Cross II

    Dayna Hubenthal

    Len Kovar

    Caroline Miller

    Jody Seay

    Lynn Weiss

The Path of God

www.ingramcontent.com/pod-product-compliance
Lightning Source LLC
LaVergne TN
LVHW020926090426
835512LV00020B/3226